CHARLES R. KINGHAN

RENDERING TECHNIQUES

FOR COMMERCIAL ART AND ADVERTISING

REINHOLD PUBLISHING CORPORATION

NEW YORK

Second Printing, 1964

Reinhold Publishing Corporation

Printed in U. S. A.

Library of Congress Catalog Card Number: 57-9461

To my wife, Ruth, whose patience, understanding and help have made it possible for me to write this book.

The Author

Born in Anthony, Kansas, Charles R. Kinghan's first venture into the commercial art field came about in Wichita, Kansas, in 1914, where he wrote show cards and painted signs. In 1916 he started his studies at the Academy of fine arts in Chicago, Illinois, but they were interrupted when he enlisted in the Armed Services in 1917. After his discharge, he resumed his studies at the Academy, attending evening classes. Later he studied at the Art Institute and the American Academy of Art, where he also taught for some time.

In Chicago he free-lanced for many years, working on major accounts for advertising and doing some story illustrating. He was affiliated with Haddon Sundblom for several years before coming east to New York in 1937. He was co-owner and instructor of The Huguenot School of Art in New Rochelle, New York, until 1953. He has been associated with major agencies in New York City and at present is on the staff of Batten, Barton, Durstine & Osborn, Inc., certainly one of the most important advertising agencies in the country.

Mr. Kinghan is an Associate-elect of the National Academy, a member of the American Watercolor Society, Allied Artists of America, the Salamagundi Club, Pennsylvania Watercolor Club, the Hudson Valley Art Association, and past president of the New Rochelle Art Association. His membership has been fully justified by the many awards and prizes he has won for his watercolors in all the aforementioned organizations. Most recently, he received the Emily Lowe Award in the 1957 American Watercolor Society exhibition at the National Academy. His pictures have been hung in museums and private collections throughout the country, and his biography appears in the latest (1956) edition of *Who's Who in American Art*. He has also written several articles for *The Artist*, a London publication, and *American Artist* magazine.

During the Second World War Mr. Kinghan was one of three artists who formed a portrait painting project for service men and women and was flown all over the country by the Army and Navy to various hospitals to carry out this work. Over 500 charcoal heads were completed by Mr. Kinghan during this period.

Contents

(Continued on next page)

Contents (continued)

Color Plates

Foreword

Art students today are faced with the task of producing professional-looking work before they find employment. Many students, when they leave art school, have a fair knowledge of drawing from casts and figures and from life; they are familiar with oils and watercolor and their application to canvas and board. But they are in most cases denied the advantages of apprenticeship, which in past years was the step from school to working as a professional. It was my good fortune to serve as an apprentice under Charles Kinghan and other artists of his caliber in Chicago, and for that privilege I am very grateful. But today our economy, the minimum wage, and social security have made apprenticeship pretty much a thing of the past. Thus the student misses the opportunity of gaining a knowledge of his tools and how to use them from an artist long established in his field.

To fill the gap left by the disappearance of the apprentice system, Mr. Kinghan presents *Rendering Techniques for Commercial Art and Advertising*. This is a book for students who have already gained some knowledge of the essentials in art but who need an introduction to the new products, tools, and techniques in the relatively new field of commercial art.

In his book, Mr. Kinghan shows the artist what tools and materials to use and how to use them with a minimum of strokes. In the past few years I have interviewed many young and aspiring commercial artists, fresh from art school, and often I have noticed a lack of economy in rendering. In our field, one learns that it is of primary importance to make a statement in his illustration in a manner that tells the story well and pleases the viewer.

The reader will find in *Rendering Techniques* exactly what is expected of him as an artist, for Mr. Kinghan shows the artist at work and examines the procedure of producing an illustration, from the art director's rough right on through to the finished art work. Also there are several sections in the book in which other prominent artists show how they approach and solve particular problems that are bound to crop up in the life of the commercial artist today.

Since apprenticeships are very hard to come by nowadays, it is my opinion that this book is very timely. I earnestly recommend it as a valuable addition to the library of the practicing commercial artist as well as to the student. *Rendering Techniques* is not a book to be simply read once and then put away; it is more — it is a book to be referred to again and again when specific problems confront the artist.

COLBY WHITMORE
Illustrator

Introduction

It has often been said that a building is no stronger than its foundation. The simple principle of this well-worn phrase could be applied to any field of endeavor, and particularly to commercial art. A thorough familiarization with the all-over problem at hand and a basic understanding of the materials to be used are of utmost importance to an artist.

In a sense, an artist is a builder putting up a new structure with each assignment he faces. The foundation must be solid if the job is to be a sound one. An artist must start from the beginning, with a plan. As a builder, he must be absolutely certain of his materials, for they are his tools. It is essential that the artist master and understand each one, get them to work for him and not against him. *Rendering Techniques*, therefore, is primarily concerned with these tools and their use and application to the commercial field.

In the advertising field an artist must be thoroughly familiar with the requirements of his client. With each new assignment, he must plan his approach to the problem, deciding which medium and rendering technique would best put across the visual message quickly and clearly. The artist must mold all elements to tell the story of a product and blend illustrations and copy into a sound and eye-pleasing advertisement.

Of course, before an ad is seen on the printed page, it goes through a well-thought-out building process — the layout. In all major agencies there are several kinds of layouts used. First, there is the very rough indication or first rough. This first rough takes explaining to the artist and may come from the account man or art director who is handling the specific account. The next layout may be fairly well established as to subject matter and composition; it eliminates the usual guesswork on the part of the artist. A third type is the "talking rough." This layout may be carried out by either the art director or the artist who is assigned the job. The "talking rough" is carried far enough along so that the client can see approximately what the finished comprehensive will look like. The last and final step is the finished comprehensive — with all the elements either reasonably completed or slickly finished. The finished comprehensive is the closest approximation to the final printed advertisement.

In *Rendering Techniques* I have endeavored to help young artists in their approach to the commercial field and to help them build the foundation that will enable them to execute sound and visually exciting comprehensives.

The examples assembled in this book include the work of many top-flight artists and art directors, giving the young artist a well-rounded cross-section of viewpoints and stimulating ideas.

I acknowledge gratefully the aid and assistance through consultation and participation, of the art directors Harold Olsen, Robert Bode, Walter McGovern, and Lawrence Berger and of the following artists: Donald F. Moss, James A. Ernst, August Bleser, George Rapp, Seymour Ball, Rolf Klep, Patrick J. White, Henry McAlear, Edward Klauck, and Charles Hawes. Their help and enthusiasm will greatly add to the structure and foundation of many youthful careers that I hope will begin with or be aided by *Rendering Techniques*.

The Essential Tools

1. Masking Tape — holds a sheet of paper on top of your layout pad, holds the underlay or key drawing on your pad when you are ready to render your comprehensive, masks the edge of your picture area when rendering a wash drawing.
2. Red Sable Brushes — used for wash renderings and ink brush treatments ranging from wet to dry.
3. Triangle — its transparency enables you to see through it while lining the straight edges of your drawing.
4. Mat Knife — used for cutting mats, trimming the edge of your finished comprehensives, sharpening pencils.
5. Kneaded Eraser — always cut it in half — picks up pencil marks easily, leaving no erasure crumblings to brush off; by squeezing it to a sharp edge, you will be able to erase a fine line of white when working in charcoal.
6. The Stump — used for blending edges together and laying a flat tone on your paper.
7. French Curve — there are several types — will give you a true crisp line, as illustrated on page 56; always have at least two in different sizes.
8. Thumb Tacks — flat heads are the best; for general use, however, the long headed aluminum tacks are very useful too.
9. Scratch Pad — its sandpaper surface is excellent for sharpening pencils to desired points.
10. Gummed Tape — used in stretching bond paper, as illustrated on page 27.
11. Stylus — a metal rod, somewhat like a pencil lead, inserted into a handle, used for tracing your drawing onto another sheet of paper or drawing board. Simply rub a soft pencil over the second sheet, then with a bit of cotton saturated in rubber cement thinner, wipe the rubbed pencil area.
12. Graphite Stick — used when you want a large area covered quickly in one flat tone with no overlap lines showing.
13. T-Square — the steel T-square is the best — can be used as a straight edge for cutting and is less apt to get out of square.
14. Ruler — the 18-inch size is the most practical to use.
15. India Ink — used for pen, brush, and drawing instruments.
16. Gray Pastels— in several values, for black and white rendering.
17. Pastels — set of 48 ideal for your color rendering.
18. Watercolors — the individual pans are best, can easily be replenished by using tube colors; watercolors are used on your color renderings for the effects not possible in pastel.
19. Compass— used for making circles and curves — with ink or a pencil.

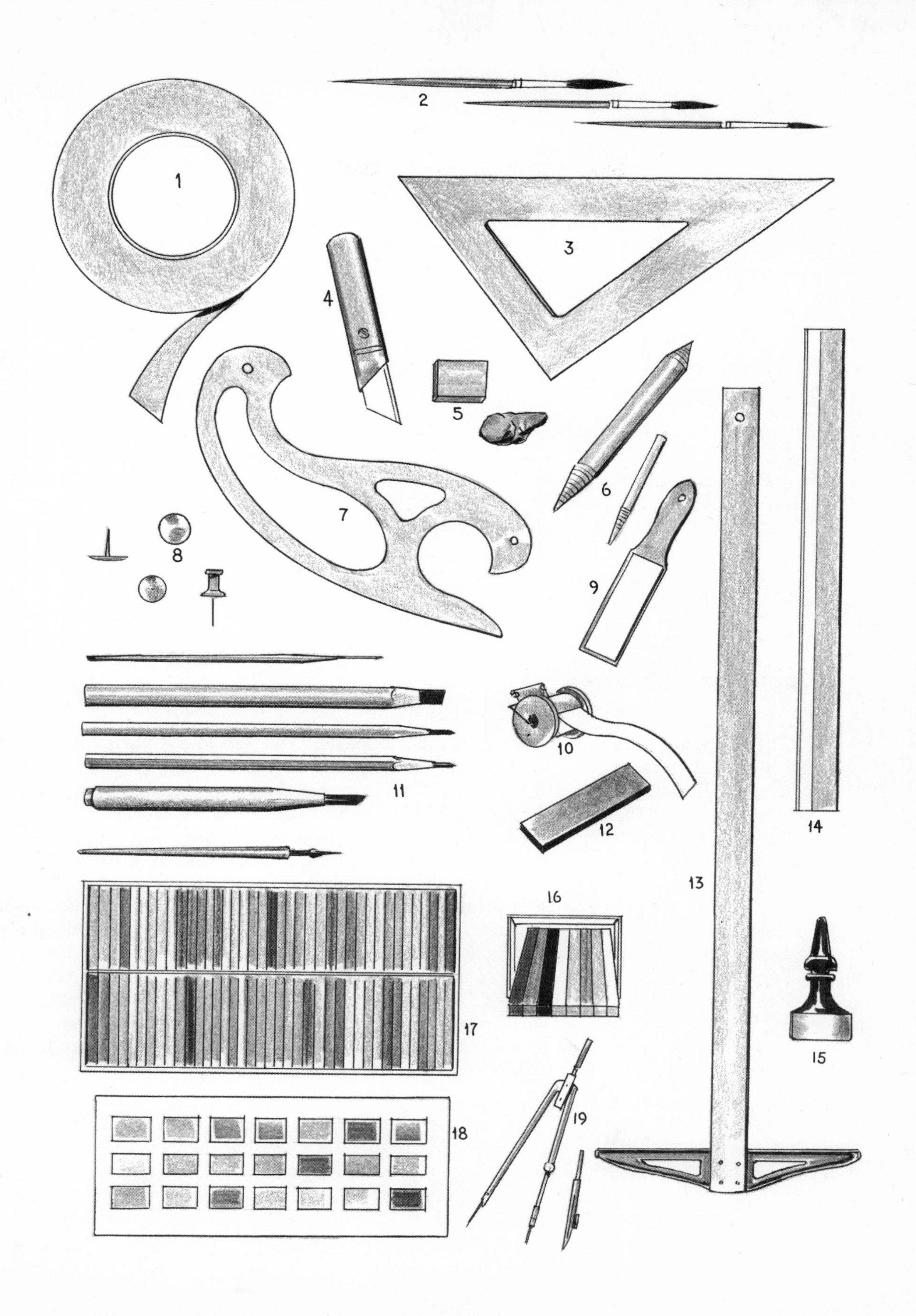
1
2
3
4
5
6
7
8
9
10
11
12
13
14
15
16
17
18
19

Chalk and Charcoal

The word chalk, as used in the trade, means pastel. You will find a variation of makes, but generally speaking the square Nupastel seems to be the one used in most agencies. I personally like them best, although there is a larger make on the market that comes in a complete set, and for some purposes I find it of great value too. The larger stick is much softer and does not have the body or pigment coverage of Nupastel. However, this again may be a matter of choice for each artist. Pastels may be purchased in different size sets, in color and from white to black, or by the single stick.

Charcoal is one of the oldest mediums used by artists. You will find it a valuable medium on certain problems in doing comprehensives. It is very pliable and is easy to pick up with a kneaded eraser. You will find that it does the least damage to the white surface of the paper when erasing. However, it must be the best grade that you can buy. I recommend a French charcoal by the name of "Fusian" — it has excellent all-round quality. Many other grades are either too soft or too hard and have a tendency to be grainy. Another type of charcoal is the kind which comes in a round stick and is used in a large holder — the same holder that is used with round graphite leads.

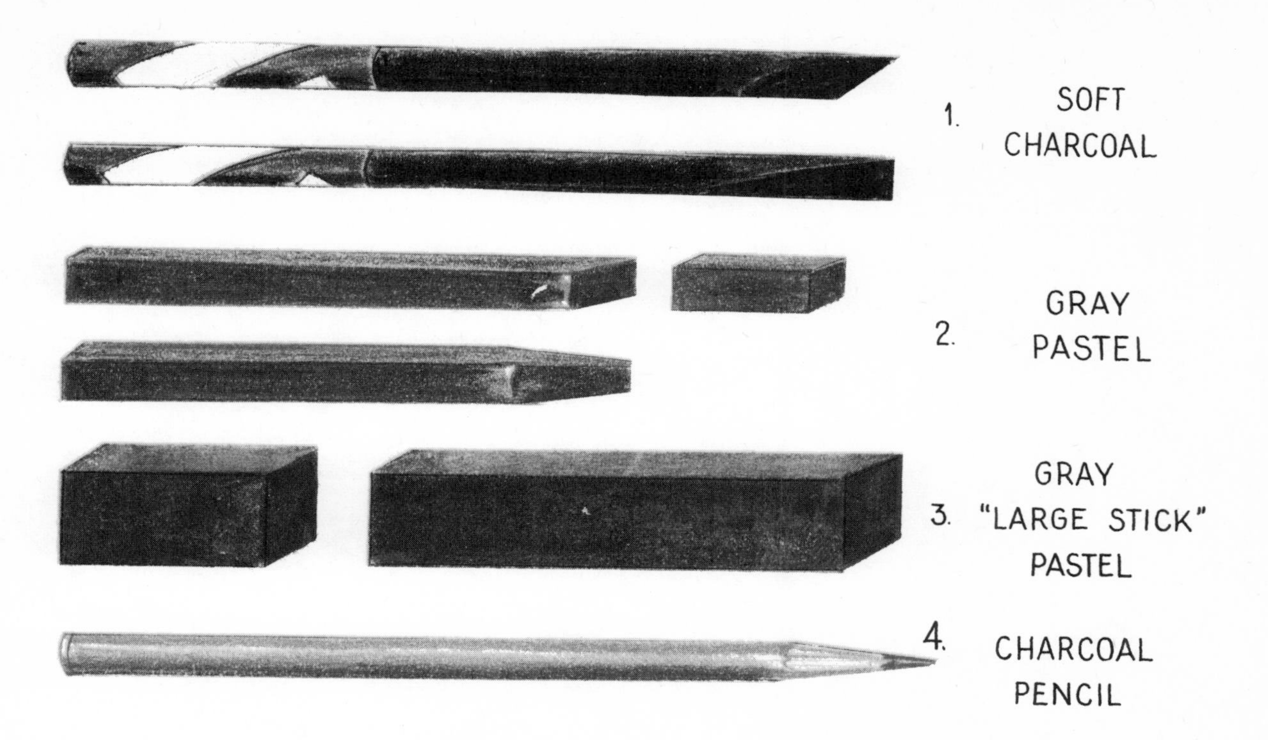
1. SOFT CHARCOAL
2. GRAY PASTEL
3. GRAY "LARGE STICK" PASTEL
4. CHARCOAL PENCIL

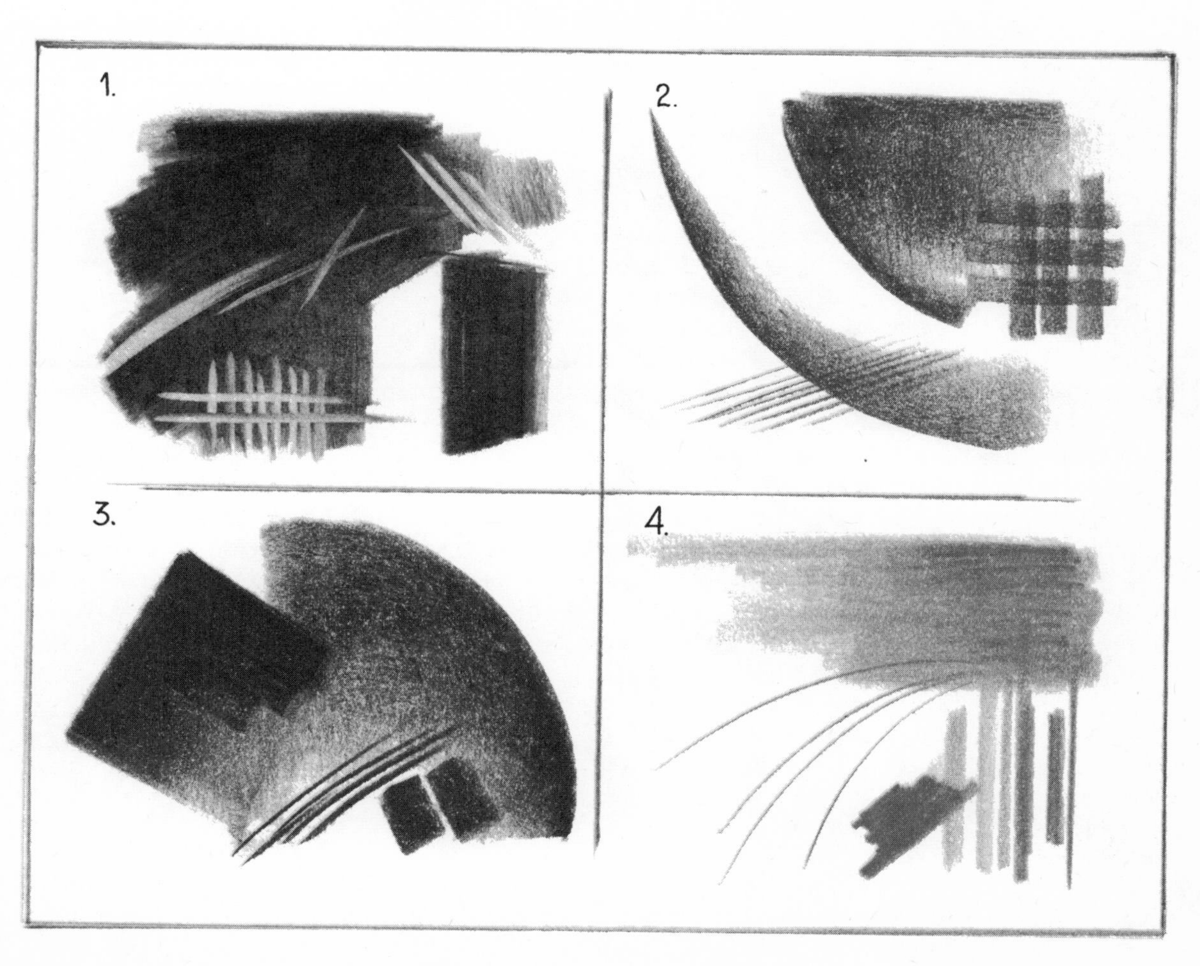
1.
2.
3.
4.

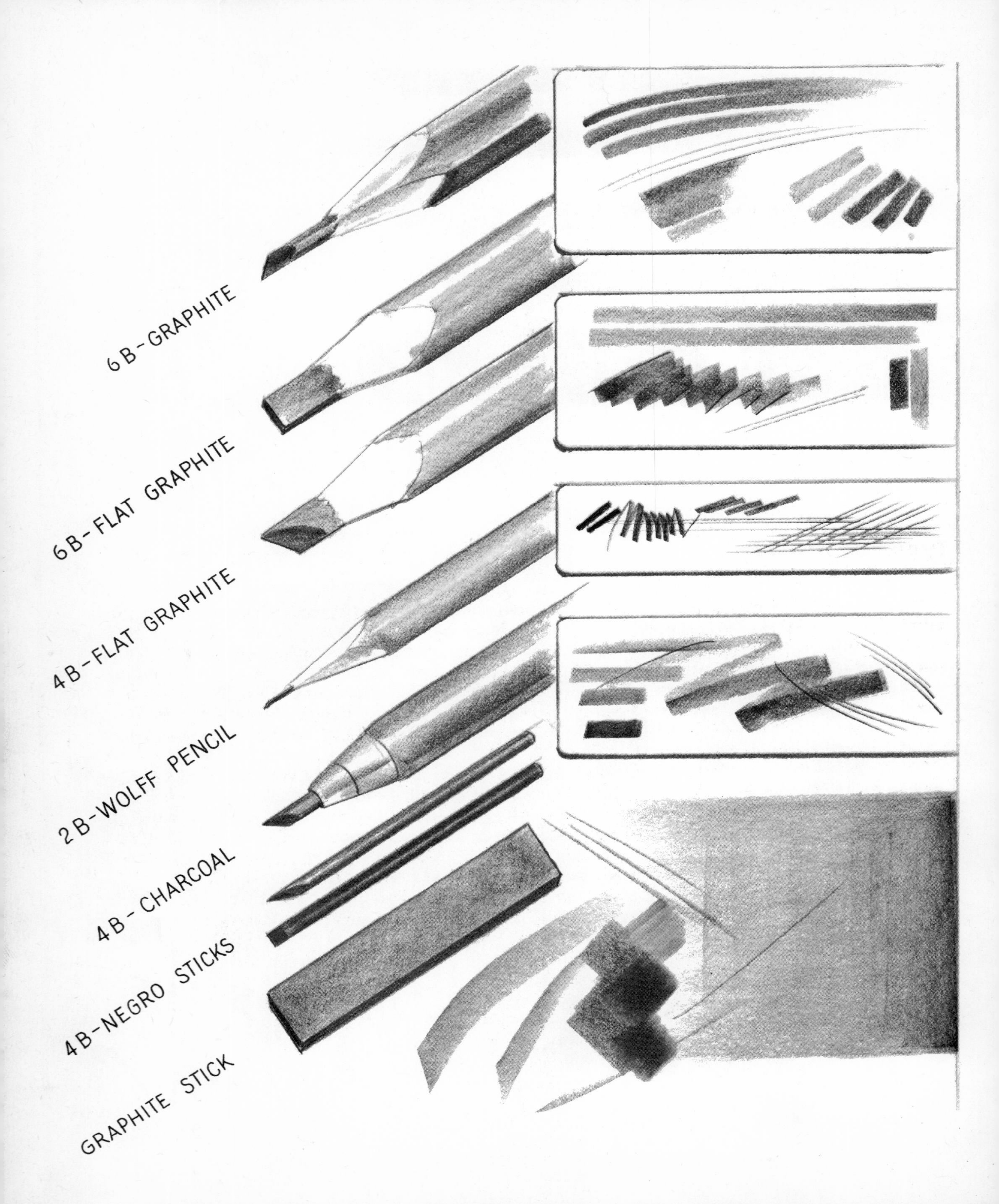
6B-GRAPHITE
6B-FLAT GRAPHITE
4B-FLAT GRAPHITE
2B-WOLFF PENCIL
4B-CHARCOAL
4B-NEGRO STICKS
GRAPHITE STICK

Types of Pencils

Pencils come in a wide variation of makes but I prefer the Venus or Eagle pencil because it is less apt to break at the point. The flat carpenters type of pencil has many uses — you can cover a large flat area in a hurry and get a rich black effect where it is needed. By sharpening the pencil in different points you can achieve a variety of uses and effects in pencil renderings.

Other graphite pencils will vary with the purpose for which they are used. I use an HB or H to establish my drawing outline before I go on with value — keeping my line clean and accurate. However, this pencil is not used in establishing the key drawing for a pastel rendering because pastel will slip and not cover over the pencil.

The Wolff pencil is a most valuable tool. I use it when rendering an automobile or any other mechanical subject matter. It is also useful in sharpening up accents, like the details in a face. If, for instance, you have been rendering a figure in gray chalks, use the Wolff pencil to finish up with, after the big values have been clearly established. It is best to have several of the same type of pencil sharpened to the desired shape before starting any particular job. Sharpen the pencils with your razor blade mat knife — it will give your pencils a clean, sharp edge.

The Graphite Flat Stick, which is about one inch by three inches by an eighth of an inch thick, is best for covering large areas quickly. It is valuable for quick indications in layouts — giving the illusion that a lot more is happening than actually is.

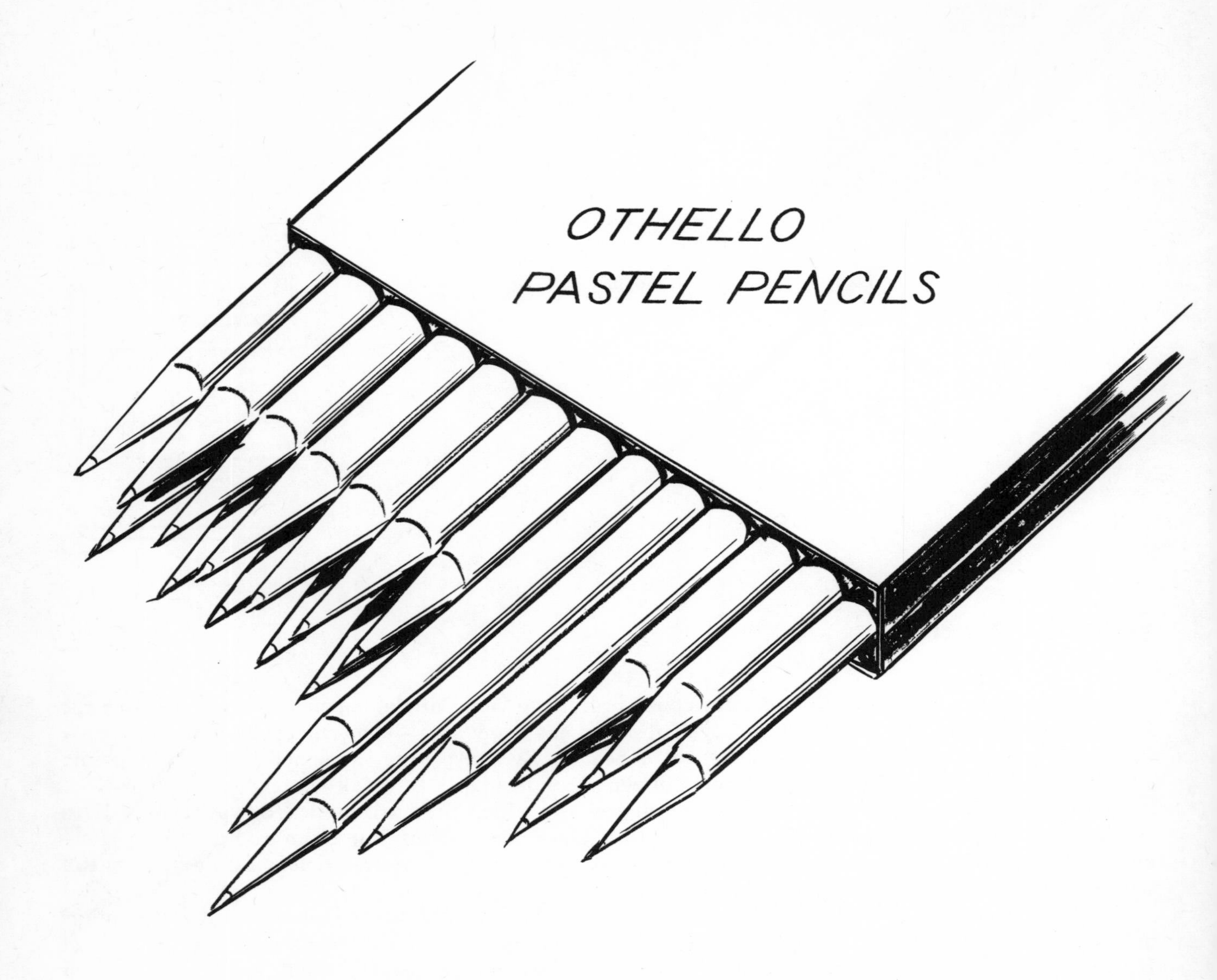

The PASTEL PENCIL is a relatively new art tool. It is of great help when rendering a small head or figure. With the use of a scratch pad, you can get a very fine point on the pencil. The pencil does not have the body or density of the square pastel stick; however, it does have its advantages and has a place among your mediums.

The CADO (FLO-MASTER) PEN is a medium widely used by artists. It is very useful in first roughs as it works well on bond paper, is very fast and will produce a very soft tone or a very rich black one. It will not rub or smear and it dries immediately. It can be filled with a special ink by removing the top portion. The felt points come in several different shapes which can be inserted as needed in the mouth of the pen. These points are used in many ways. This pen is also fine for sketching freely and quickly.

Methods of Enlarging and Reducing

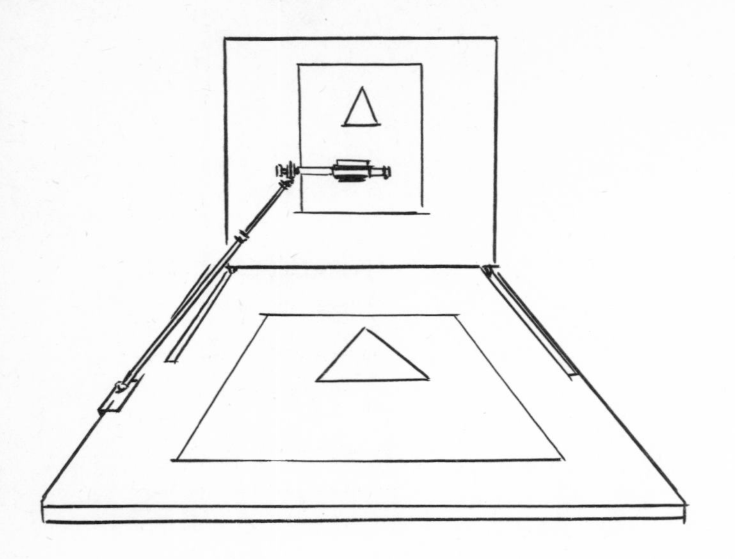

1. The CAMERA-LUCIDA is the most commonly used in enlarging. An adjustable rod is attached to a table. Looking through a prism-glass that is placed on the small arm gives you an image tacked on the upright board. This board is movable to allow you to adjust for size. Looking down on your pad you see the enlarged image and by following what you see, you pencil in to size.

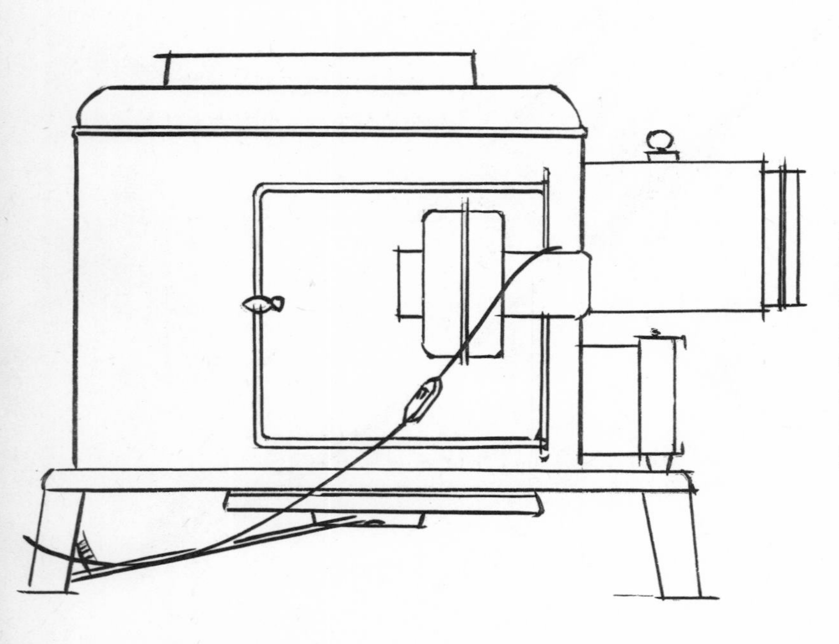

2. The BELL OPTICAN is sometimes used to enlarge a small drawing up to ten or twelve feet wide. Its one disadvantage is that the drawing to be enlarged cannot be over six inches in size. Other types, which will take a larger size sketch, are more advisable to have. These, however, are more expensive than the rod-type or camera-lucida.

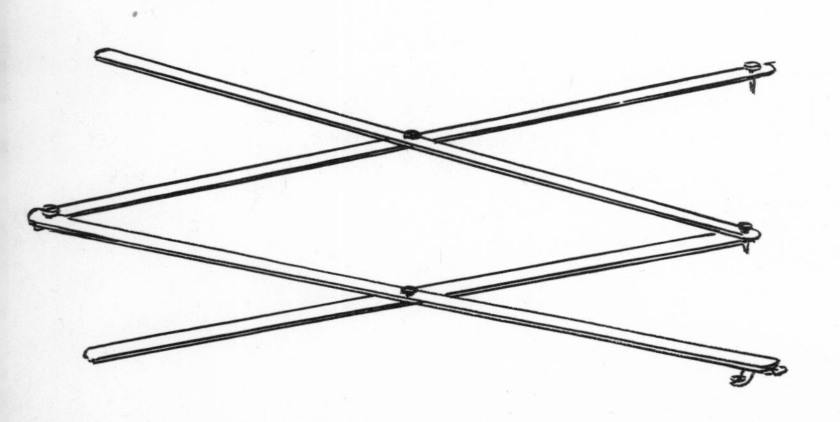

3. The PANTOGRAPH is a criss-cross device with one end thumb-tacked down. It will either enlarge or reduce most subject matter, and directions come with each one.

The "LAZY LUCY" is a rather large machine used in most agencies because of its size and scope. It will take a full-size magazine page, enabling you to enlarge any part of it. This machine is quite expensive and is about five feet high by five feet long. It has four light shades with which to light the subject matter.

Layout Pads

TRANSPARENT TISSUE PAD. This pad is used when tracing some object from a photograph or some previously rendered material. It is also used when mounting a panel onto a layout. This is done by placing a sheet of the transparent paper over the cemented area you are to mount, leaving about one-half inch of the cemented area exposed at the top. This shows you the pencil line you have to follow and you will be able to see just where to place the object you are mounting. Then, after pressing the top portion of the panel in place, slip the tracing paper down as you continue pressing the mounting onto the cemented area. This procedure eliminates any wrinkles. Then as your last step, pick up any surplus edges of the cement with your rubber cement "pick-up."

SEMI-TRANSPARENT PAD. This pad is thinner than a heavy bond paper pad and heavier than the transparent pad. However, it is transparent enough to see through when you slip a pencil drawing under one of its sheets. This type of paper allows corrections and refinements of drawing done on the transparent pad. It is used for making your key drawing.

HEAVY BOND PAD. There are many kinds of bond layout pads on the market, but as in any other material, always get the best. You should use first-grade bond to render any comprehensive. It is reasonably tough, has the right surface, and the color is brilliant white, unlike cheaper bond paper.

Rubber Cement

Rubber cement is a necessity in any art department. It is used to mount mats on a finished comprehensive, to mount a cut-out part of any layout like a rendered illustration, logotype, bits of copy or any other object desired in an ad. To mount bond paper, rubber cement should be thinned to the consistency of a light syrup; for mats, a heavier consistency is required, and the rubber cement should be as thick as molasses. An air tight jar is one of the best ways to maintain the proper consistency. For permanent adhesion, always cement both objects before mounting. A "pick-up" can be made by allowing a glob of rubber cement to dry and then kneading it into the right shape.

Fixative

There are many kinds of fixative on the market, but the most convenient kind is the "non-glossy" type. This has no shine at all. Always apply the first coat lightly and let it dry before applying a second coat for fixing permanency. With this type of fixative on a pastel, you may use white or other opaque colors to true up the details after it is completely dry.

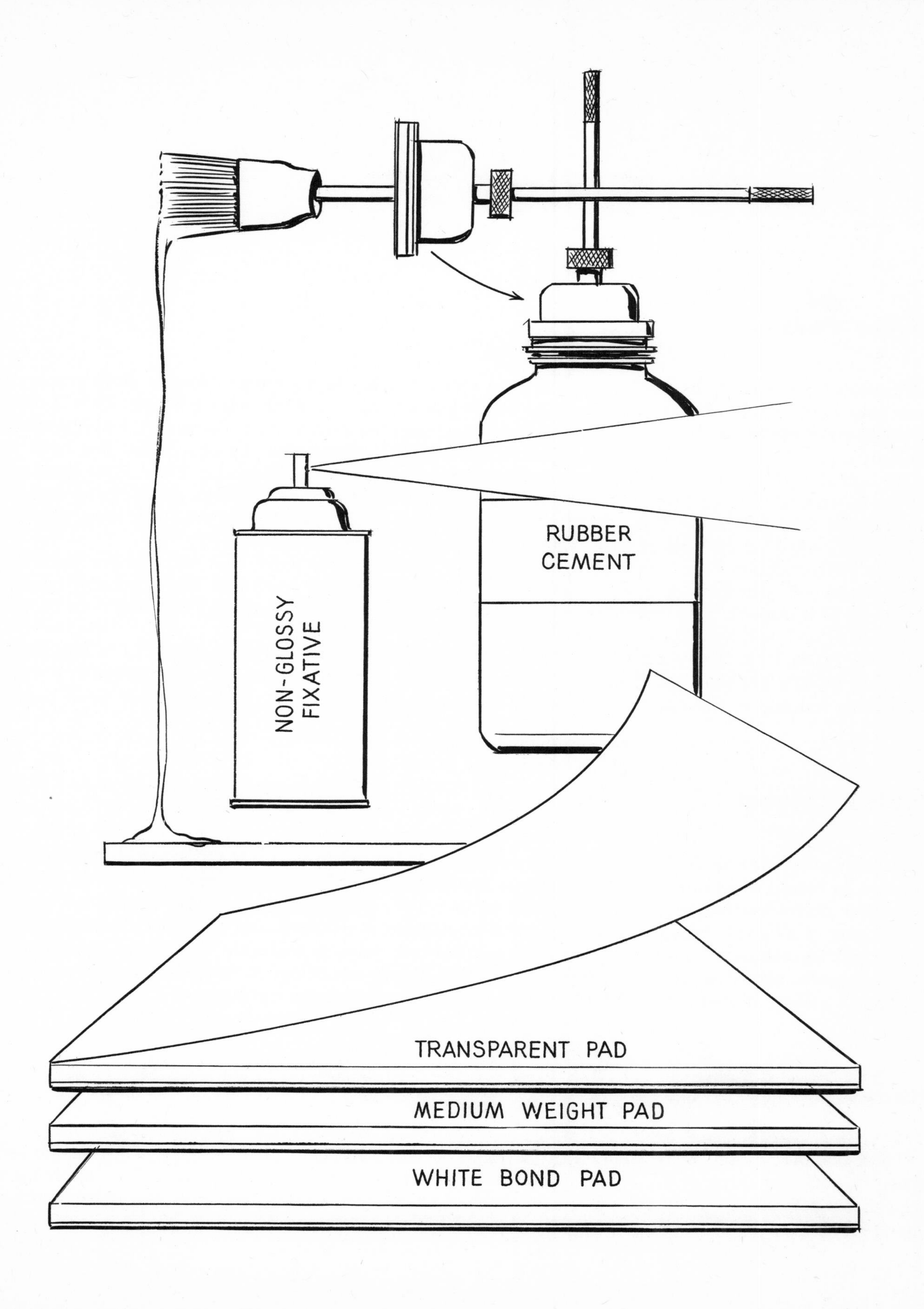
RUBBER
CEMENT
NON-GLOSSY
FIXATIVE
TRANSPARENT PAD
MEDIUM WEIGHT PAD
WHITE BOND PAD

Simple Perspective

Whenever you have a rendering problem involving an interior, such as a room with furniture, the first thing to decide is how much of the ceiling should show and at what angle the floor line should be drawn. Illustrated on the next page is an example of how to find your horizon line. Carry the floor line and the ceiling line out to their vanishing point on one side of the drawing. By extending a line across the sheet through the vanishing point, you establish the horizon line. Any object placed within the room must start somewhere along this line. The vanishing points of the objects drawn within the room may move to any place along this line, depending on where you want the object placed — either parallel with the wall or at an angle to the wall. Build from the floor up. Draw the furniture or objects in the room as squares, oblongs, or whatever shape is desired on the floor plane. Use your triangle for the uprights.

If you find that the vanishing point is off your drawing board, move your drawing to one edge of the board, enough so that you can, for the moment, arrive at your horizon line. Then center your pad again and turn to page 24 for your next step, the perspective arc, which outlines a simple way of bringing your vanishing point onto your board. The perspective arc is easily and simply made. It is a valuable time-saver and will enable you to operate within the limits of your drawing board and not halfway across the room.

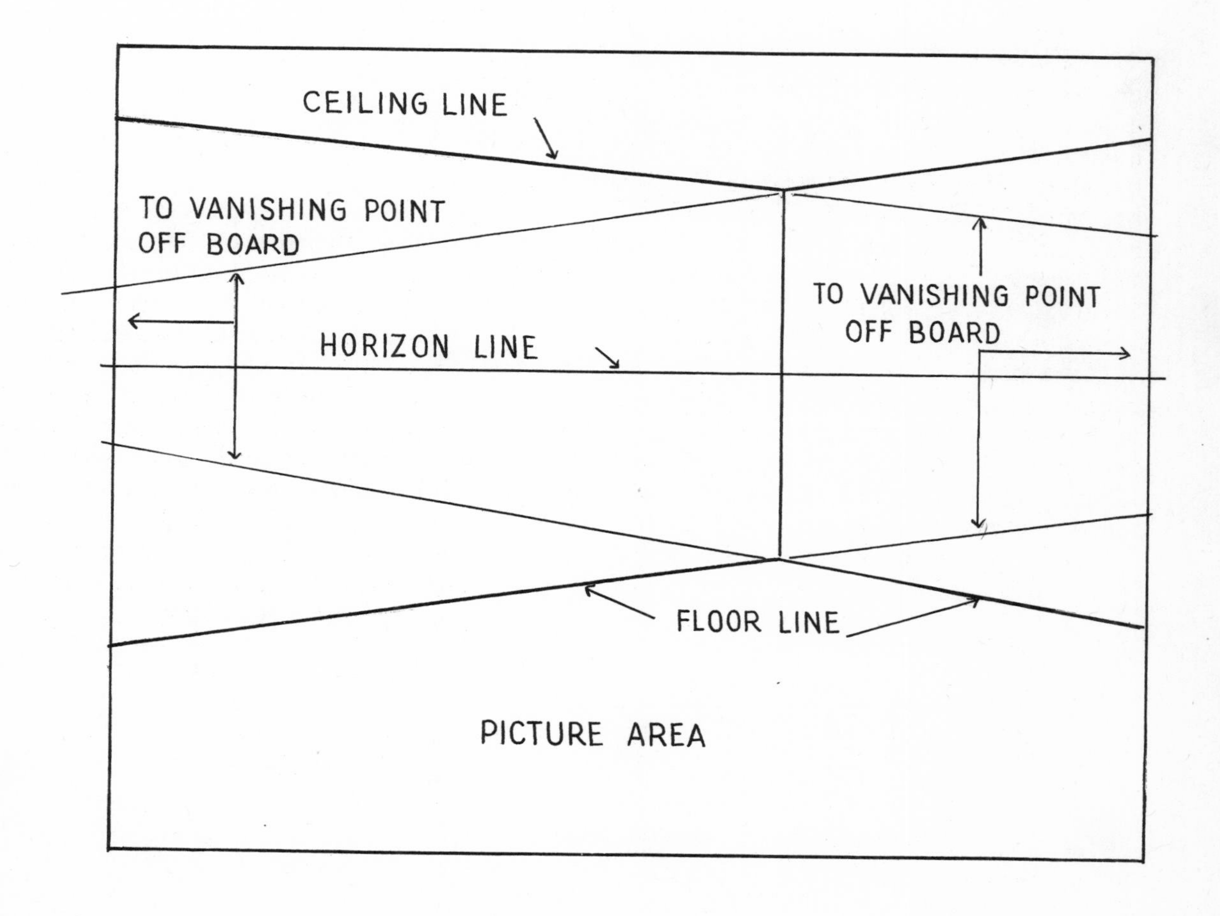
CEILING LINE
TO VANISHING POINT
OFF BOARD
TO VANISHING POINT
OFF BOARD
HORIZON LINE
FLOOR LINE
PICTURE AREA

The Perspective Arc

Cut three six-inch-wide strips of cardboard the length of a layout pad; then make a two-inch-wide strip of cardboard, 30 inches long. Secure one end of the two-inch-wide strip onto your board with a thumbtack. Make a small hole in the other end of the strip and insert the point of a pencil through it. By using the thumbtack as a pivot, you can draw an arc on one of the six-inch-wide strips. Cut along the line of this arc to make the perspective arc. To make the other two perspective arcs, each with a different degree of curvature, move the pivotal thumbtack along the two-inch-wide strip as desired.

THE THUMBTACK TRICK. In case you find a vanishing point that comes within the picture area, cut a piece of Scotch tape about an inch wide and insert a flat-headed thumbtack through the center of the tape so that the gum side of the tape is against the inside of the head of the tack. Then place the tack, point up, over the spot where the vanishing point is on the horizon line. The point of the tack is the vanishing point of your drawing and, with the Scotch tape holding the tack in place on the board, it will be well anchored for you to place a ruler or triangle against it for your lines.

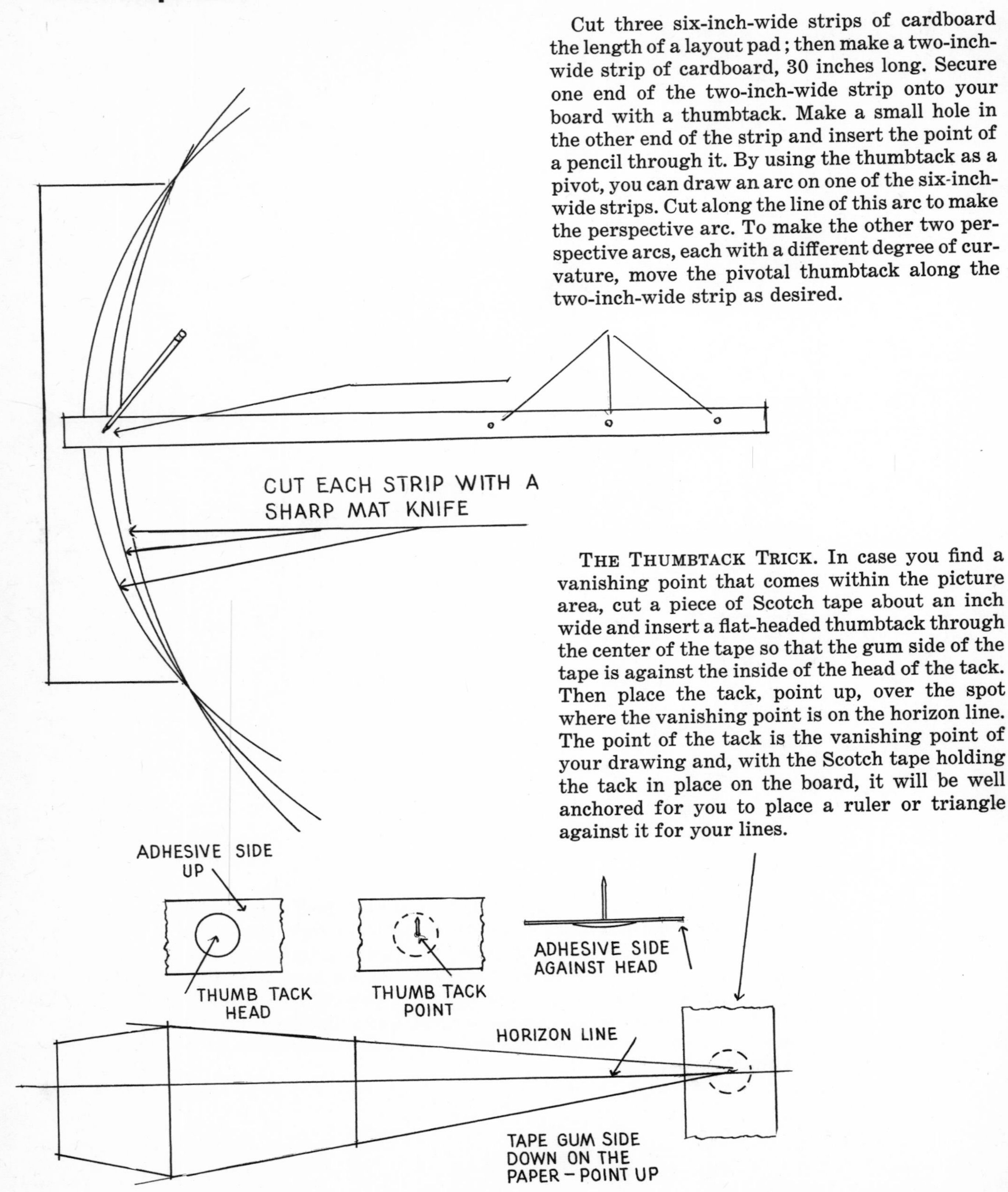

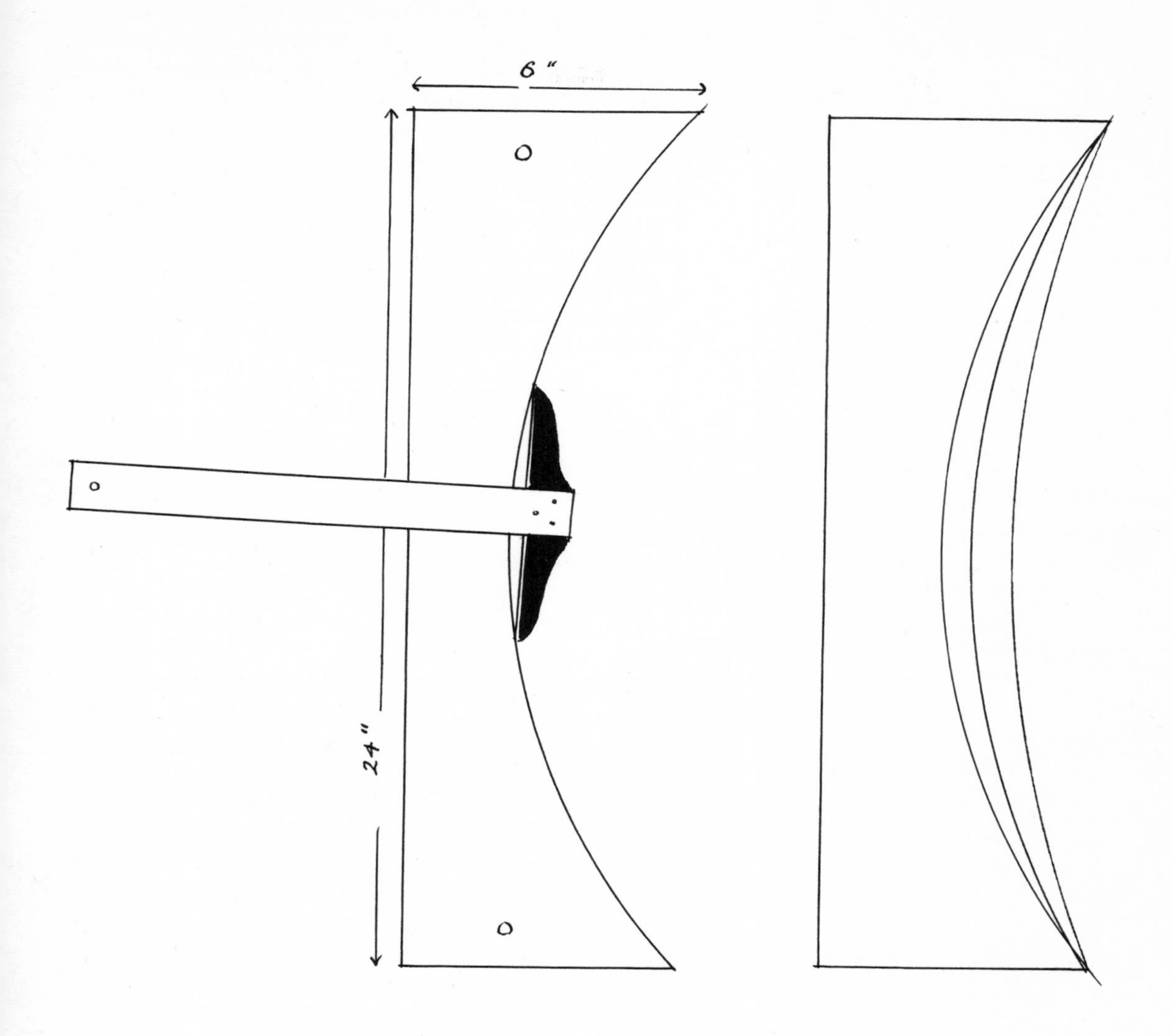

The illustration at the left above shows you how the T-square will ride along the edge of the arc. The illustration at the right shows the three degrees of circles to be drawn and then cut out. On the following page, you will see how to use the arc. Once you have tried this method, you will find it a great short-cut in establishing a fairly accurate perspective. When I lay out a room, I establish the complete room, then I find my horizon line and correct my perspective with this handy method.

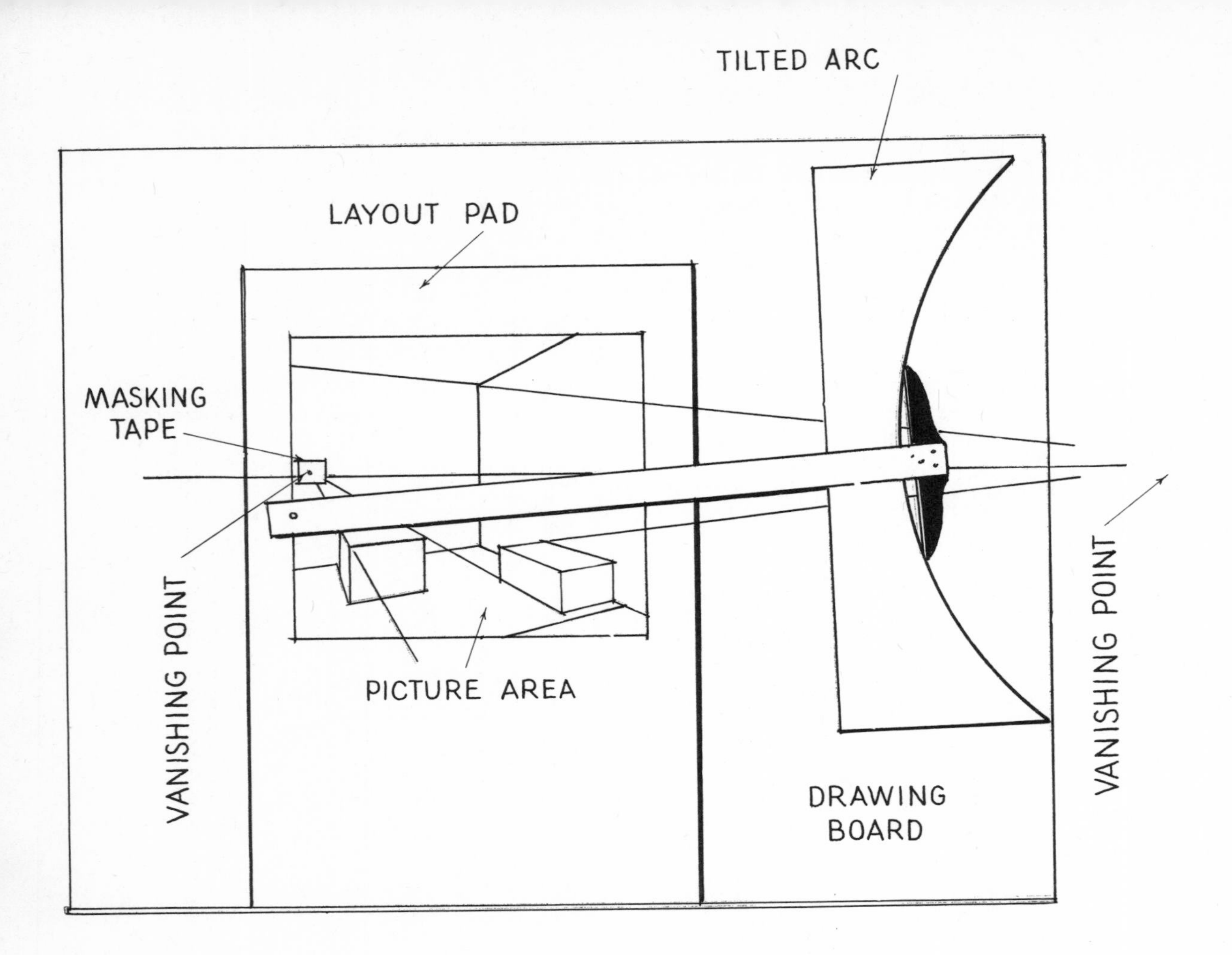

Here is how to set the arc next to your drawing, ready for use. Notice that the arc is at a slight angle, just off the perpendicular. Start with the T-square on the horizon line and move the arc either away from the drawing or toward the drawing. When the perspective arc is in its correct position, the T-square, when moved down from the horizon line, will fall along the floor line. With the perspective arc in this same position, the T-square will, when moved up on the sheet, fall along the ceiling line. Once the position of the arc is set, use a flat-headed tack and anchor your arc to the board.

Stretching Bond Paper

Cut your paper to the size desired and cut strips of gummed tape long enough to hold the paper in place. Wet the paper on the front and place it on a white board. Wet the tape and place it on all four edges of the paper. This should be done quickly; make sure there is not too much water on the paper edge or the paper will not adhere to the tape. When dry, the bond paper will be perfectly flat. As a last step, mount a piece of paper on the back of your stretched bond to prevent it from buckling.

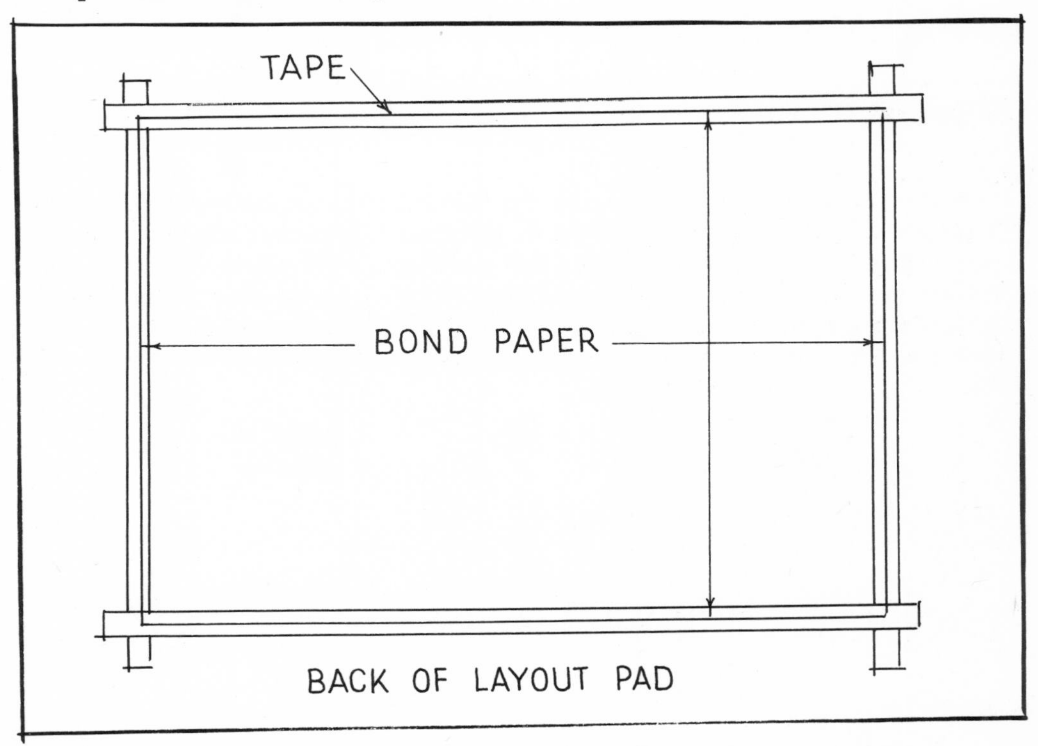

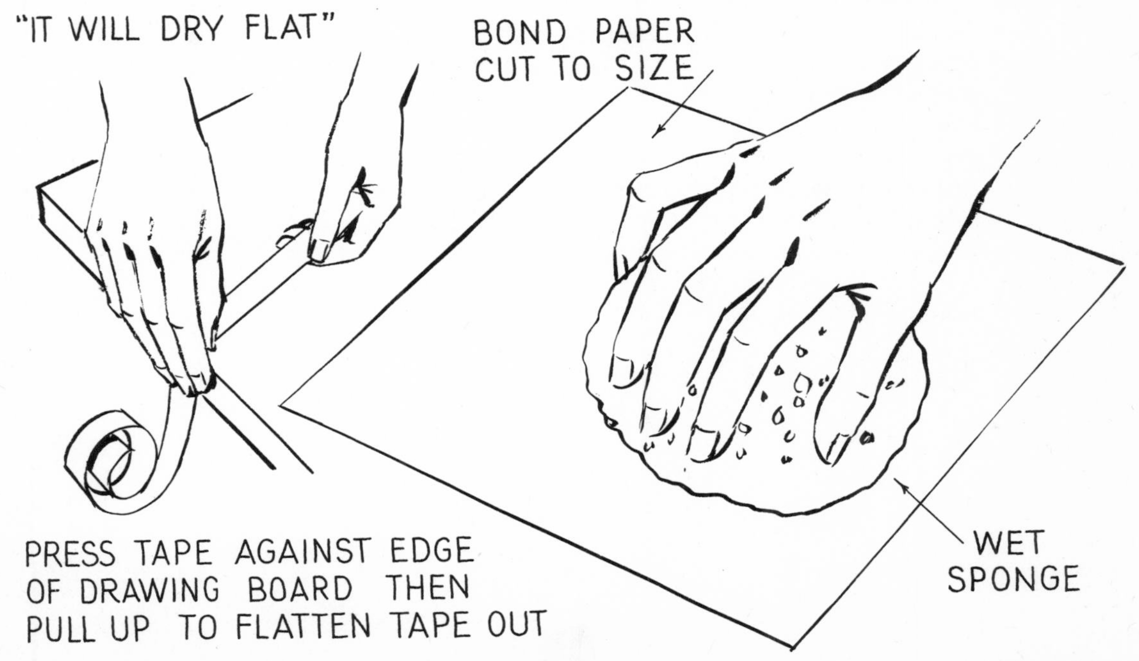

Ellipses

There are several mechanical aids for making ellipses, and you will find that the best of these are the plastic guides that can be purchased in almost any size you need. The center line is the guide for the ellipse and helps you keep the ellipse in line when you are penciling. By keeping your pencil, either graphite or Wolff's, sharpened to a fine point, you can, with the aid of a guide, true an ellipse in a jiffy. Finely sharpened pencils also help you clean up your job in a more professional way.

Key drawing

Key drawing

Roughs

First roughs are drawn by the art director to indicate the subject and the size of the picture. They also show the space the lettering will occupy and the general density of the values. The sketch man discusses all these points with the art director before starting the key drawing. The art director must determine the quality or feel of the rendering, whether it should be light and airy or something rather bold and full-toned.

In the talking rough, the sketch is carried a little further than in the first rough by the addition of a few loose tones. Having established the key drawing, it is a simple matter for the sketch man to add the three basic tones and give it a more finished look. This type of rough serves a very important purpose. An art director's first rough in many cases is not comprehensive enough to show a client; yet the client is not always quite sure what he wants; so the talking rough is used as a means of deciding. Once the decisions are made, the finished comprehensive is executed.

Above is an actual rough given to me for rendering. Even the floor plan was indicated to help visualize the placing of the various people and furnishings. It was used for an advertisement by General Electric.

Talking rough

Art director's rough

Here is an art director's rough showing the size, space, and subject matter wanted in this rendering. As is the case in all renderings, you should refer to your clipping file for copy on sports cars, figures, etc., before starting the key drawing.

Here is the key drawing ready for rendering. This ad, one of a series for a cigarette company, was rendered in pencil. The finished art work was produced by photography.

Art director's rough, used to establish the general theme of the picture reproduced on page 107.

Key drawing

Mechanical Subjects

In rendering anything mechanical, use any device that will give the comprehensive sketch a crisp finish. The ellipse guide is a great aid in attaining a crisp, clean curve. Where you need a sharp line to give your drawing a finished look, line your edges with a triangle or a ruler. There are, of course, certain edges that should be left soft for the purposes of turning the object drawn. In any drawing not all edges should be hard, nor should they all be soft. It is the play of one against the other that gives the finished drawing a professional look.

On the next few pages you will find several subjects, rendered either completely or partially, illustrating this approach. Chalks and pencils are the materials used in these renderings. The series of photographs which begin on page 54 show the different materials and how they can be used. Study these carefully, see how to hold the pastel, pencils, etc., and make your own variations to suit your own personal needs and facilities.

Talking rough

Key drawing for underlay

Use of the Tools and Materials

In the commercial field there are tools that are absolutely essential. Each agency, studio, and artist has a variety of approaches to a rendering problem, but the tools dealt with on these pages are complete enough for the artist to handle any comprehensive problem, with the exception of an oil rendering.

As you examine each page and its problem, you will see that each article has its specific, important use. To get the most out of any example, try each one step by step, taking advantage of the hints given — the color, the medium, the pencil. Experiment with your pencils and pastels — sharpened, chiseled, flat, and round. Such experimentation adapts your own hands to a suggested method — but that method will come to you naturally and personally *only if you experiment with it.*

Remember, your finish will be no better than your drawing. See to it that your key drawing, which is placed under the bond paper for your rendering, is as well drawn as you can make it.

The importance of experimentation holds true again with the pastel stick. Become acquainted with the right way to hold it — try different strokes — see which strokes give you a direct, fresh result. The important things with pastel are freshness and spontaneity. Keep the rendering clean; if it can be done with one stroke, so much the better. Your finished result will sparkle and have no undesirable muddy qualities. It is what you leave out that counts, and not how hard you work. Overworking on a pastel can give a lot of dull, muddy values, and the skilful handling of values is the key to a well rendered drawing.

This is a partially finished drawing, showing the use of the Wolff pencil for lining the car. For the values, use the gray chalks, as illustrated in the photos of the hands on pages 54 to 63. You will find that in fixing the drawing, all values or tones will darken somewhat, so plan accordingly and apply them a little lighter than you intend in the finished work to compensate for this variance of value.

Key drawing

Photostat from which drawing was traced

1928 Hudson. Whether the car is old or brand-new, a crisp rendering is always possible with the correct usage of your material.

1922 Maxwell. By glamorizing this model and giving it sweep, the artist immediately made the car look much newer.

Here are three different subjects rendered with graphite pencils. A 2-B pencil, sharpened to a chisel point, was used for the outlines; a T-square, an ellipse guide, and a French curve were used where necessary to give a clean crisp edge.

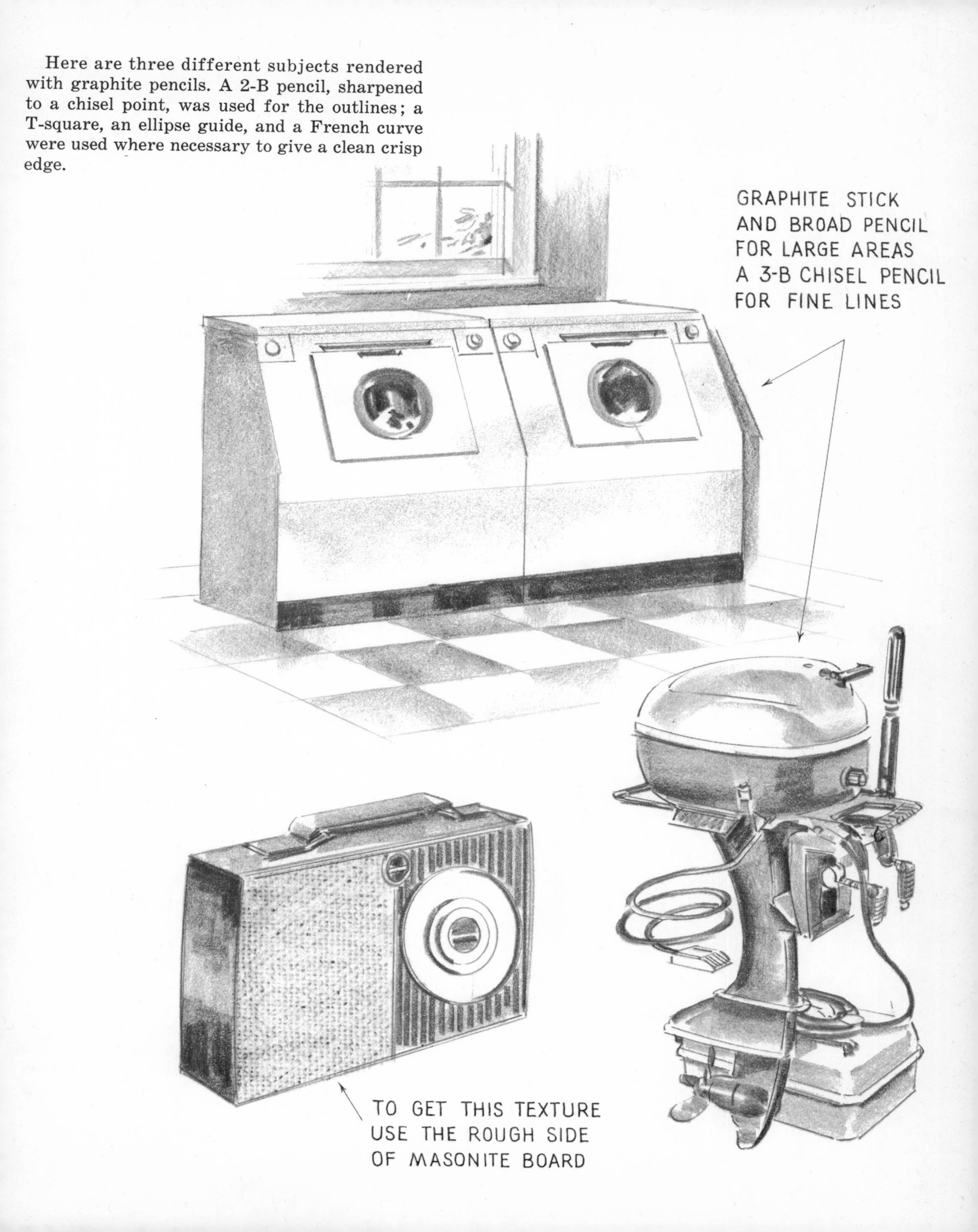

Here you may try out your perspective and the flat graphite pencil stick. Use your 3-B chisel point for the lining of the furniture and a 5-B for the dark accents.

Here it was necessary to show the full range of values but it was not necessary to do a tight drawing with a great deal of exact detail. This is the first step; next, the sketch man will render it in whatever medium is decided upon.

On the following page is a rendering of a truck executed in charcoal. This medium is very pliable and fun to work with because you can get an all-over tonal quality very fast. It is easily picked up with the kneaded eraser where you need a fine line of white. After a first application of fix, you can go back and apply another tone if you wish.

Handling Pastels and Pencils

The various advertising agencies do not follow the same pattern and policy in their sketch departments. Some present to their clients a rough art director's rendering; others will finish the ad to the extent that in some cases the pictorial part may even be used as the finished art work. In this case the comprehensive is generally rendered in wash or opaque color. A great deal depends on the desires of the client.

This point will be settled between you and the art director when you are assigned the job. Generally, you are told just how far to go or how rough it is to be, but it is wise to ask all the questions before you start the rendering.

Get acquainted with your mediums. On a trial layout pad, experiment with the different chalks. The Nupastel seems to be the best for all purposes; it has good body pigment and the colors that are included in the large box will be sufficient to do almost any rendering. You will find that there are some colors that just miss being what you want, but by compromising one way or the other you will be close enough. The pastel pencils are valuable for small heads and other details and areas; they do not have the body pigment of the square pastels, but they serve the purpose. Remember that they, too, darken in color when they are fixed. You will also find that they will have a smoother look when rubbed with a finger or a tissue.

With your graphite, try dipping the end of your stump in rubber cement thinner; then apply the stump to an area you want very dark — this gives you a soft dark value. The sharpening of your pencils is a must. By doing this, you can control the width of the stroke and the sharpness of the edge.

On the following ten pages are photographs of hands using the tools and the mediums mentioned.

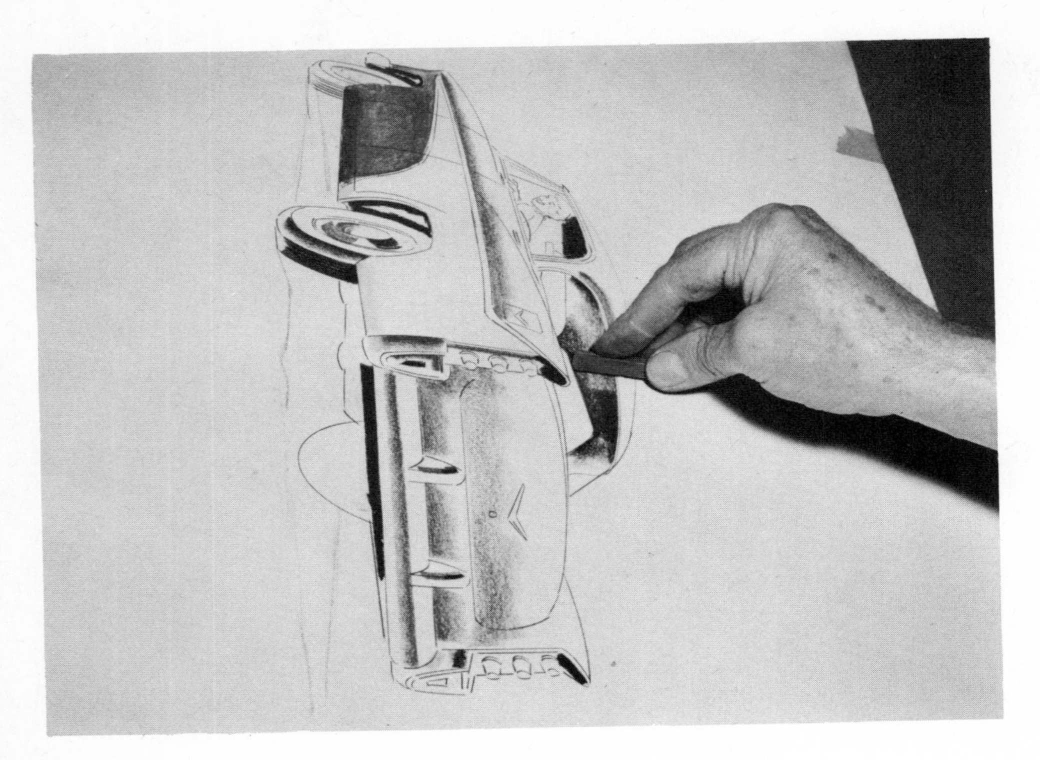

Paper turned to get at top of car

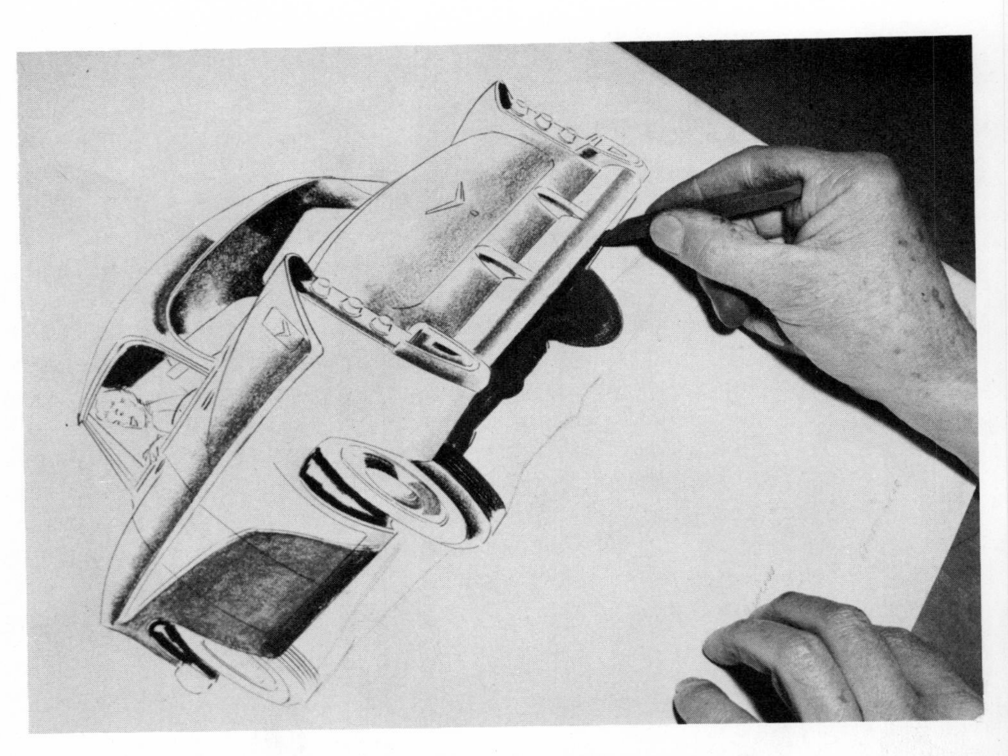

Using sharpened edge of pastel

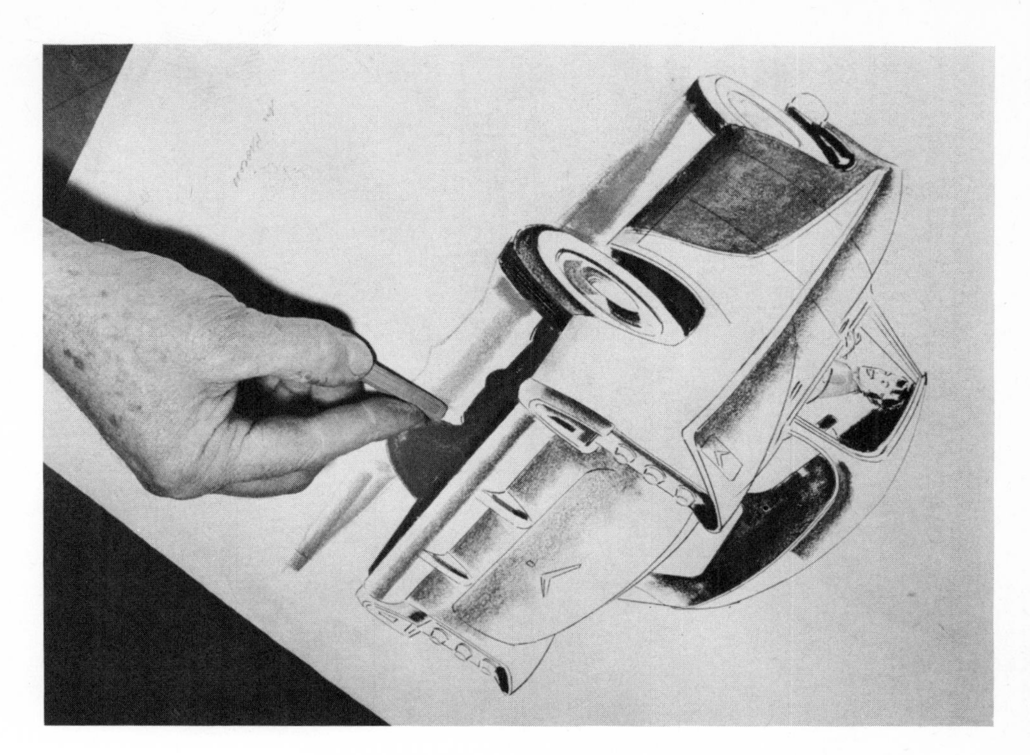

Using flat edge of pastel for shadow area

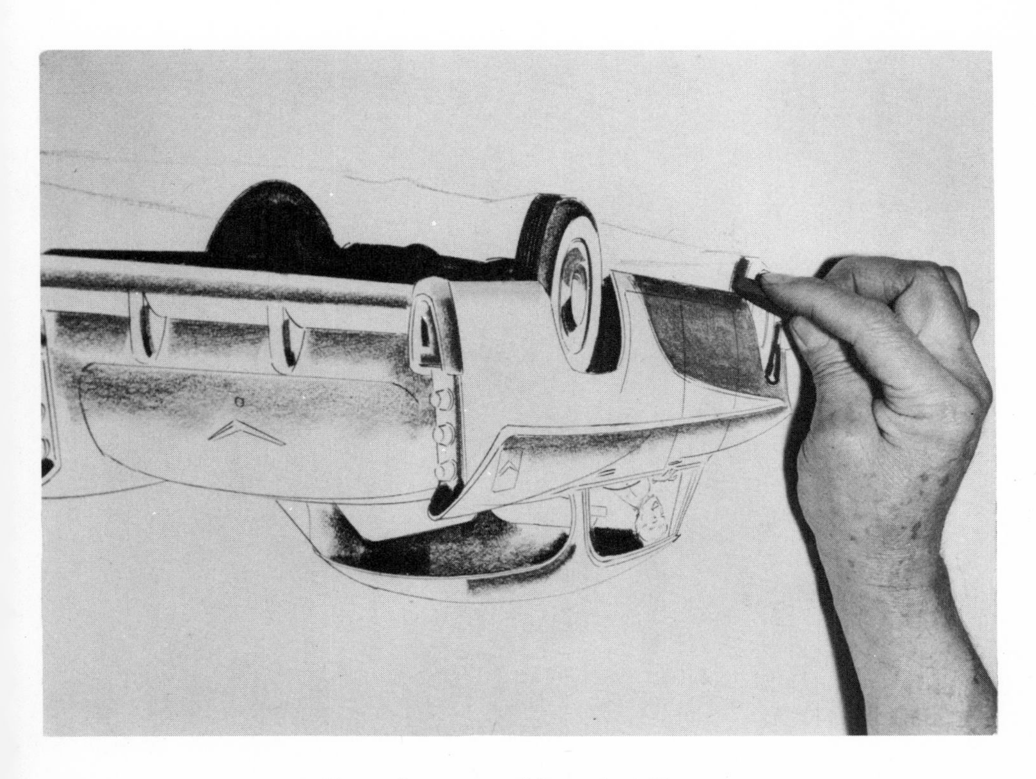

Drawing turned to get at tire

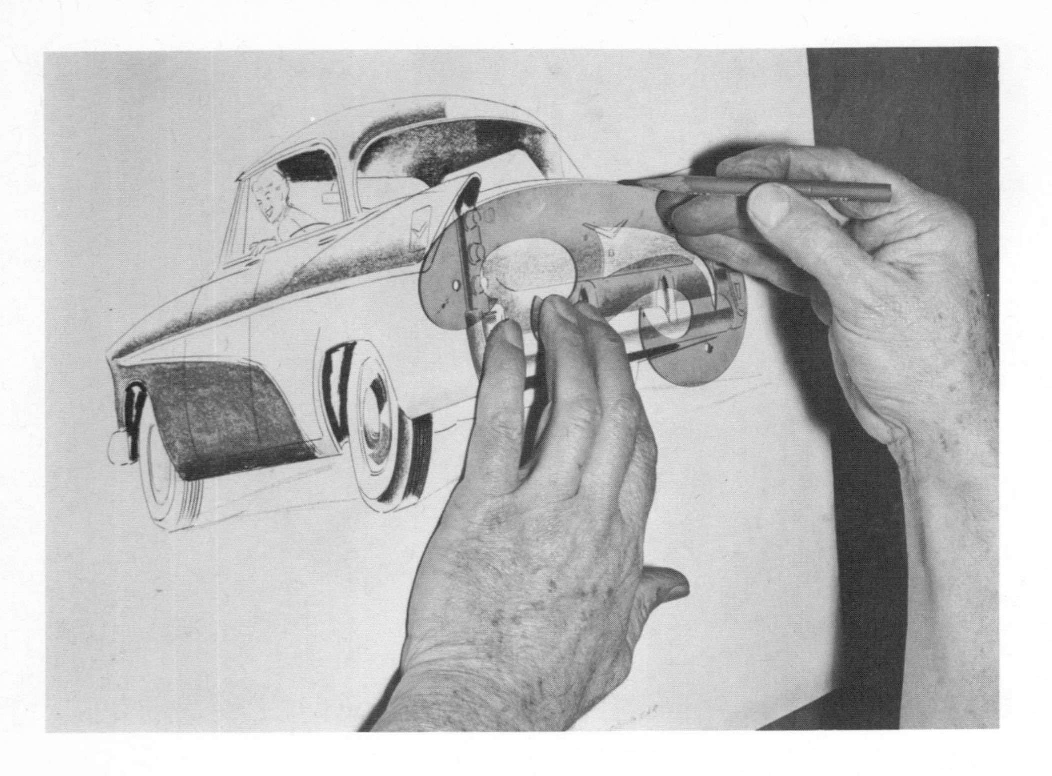

Using the French curve and Wolff pencil

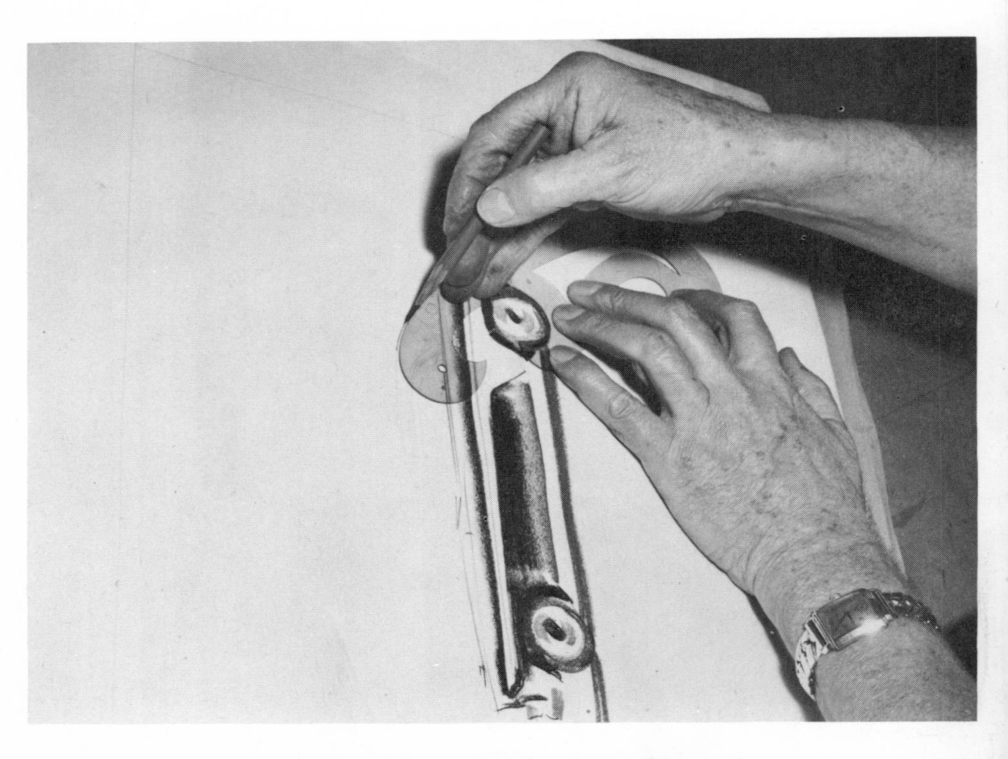

The French curve helps, even on a rough

Drawing turned for sharp edge

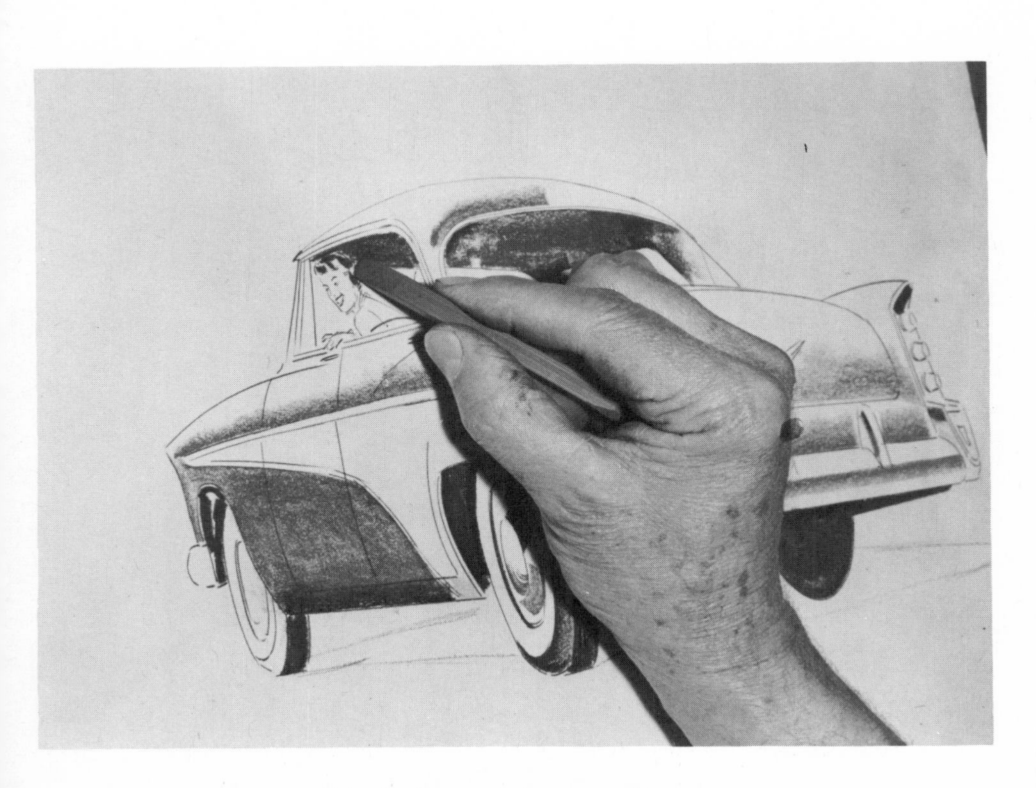

Chisel edge gets into small areas

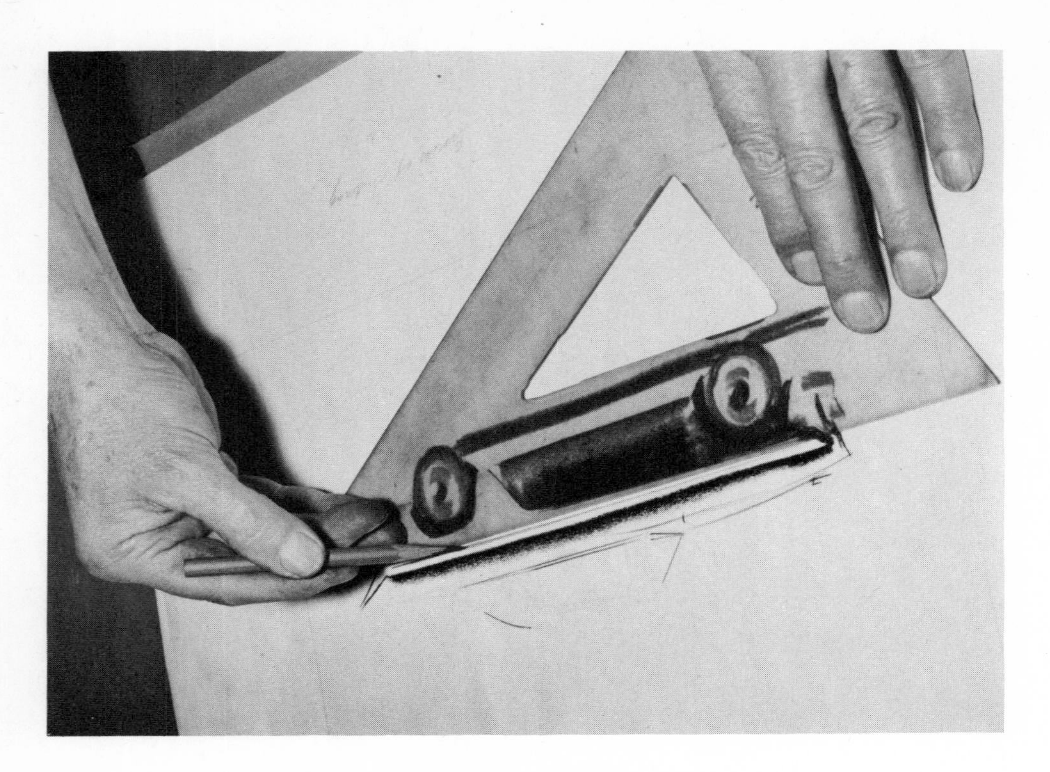

Triangle used for a sharp line

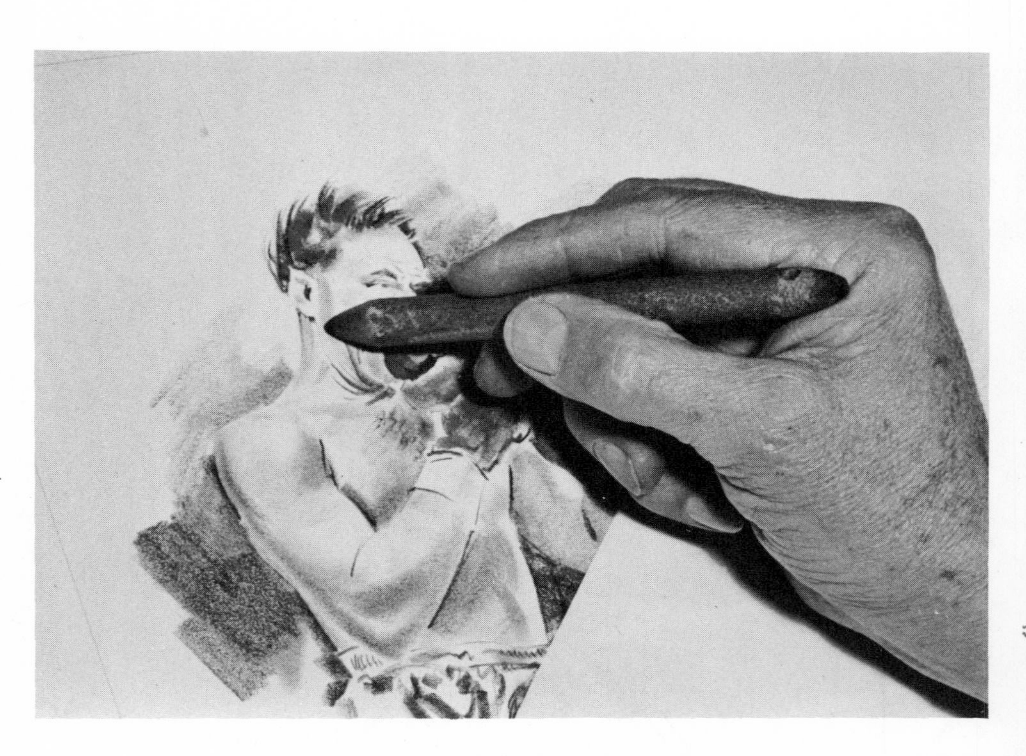

Use of the stump

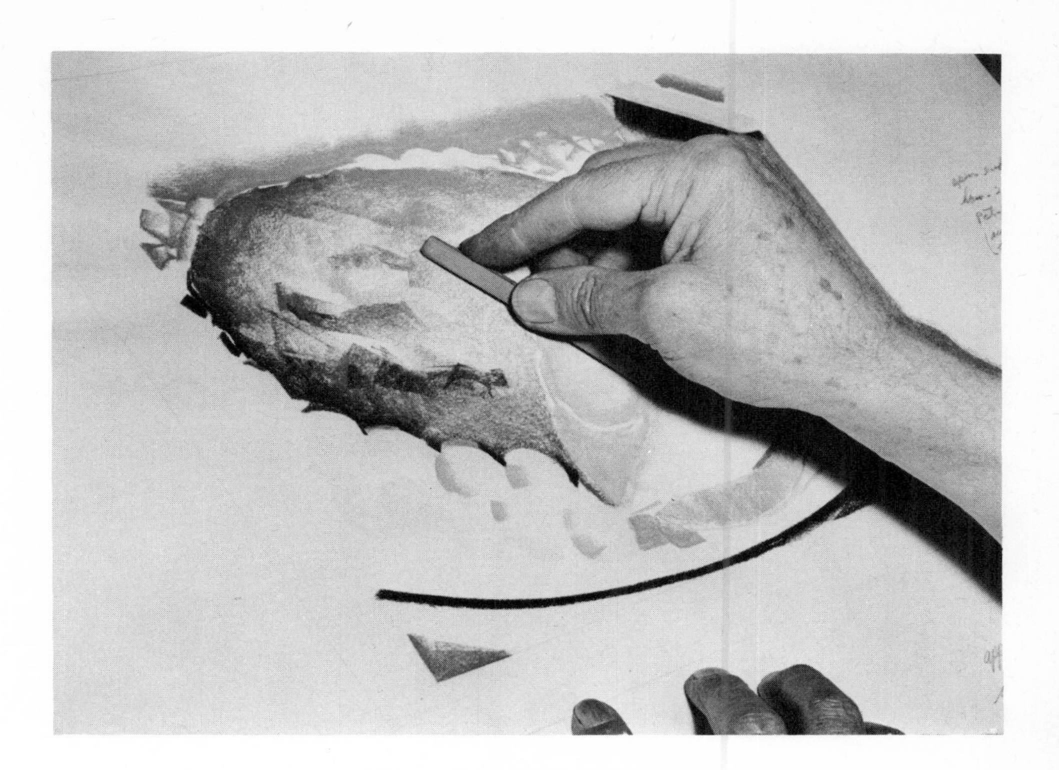

Applying the second tone on ham

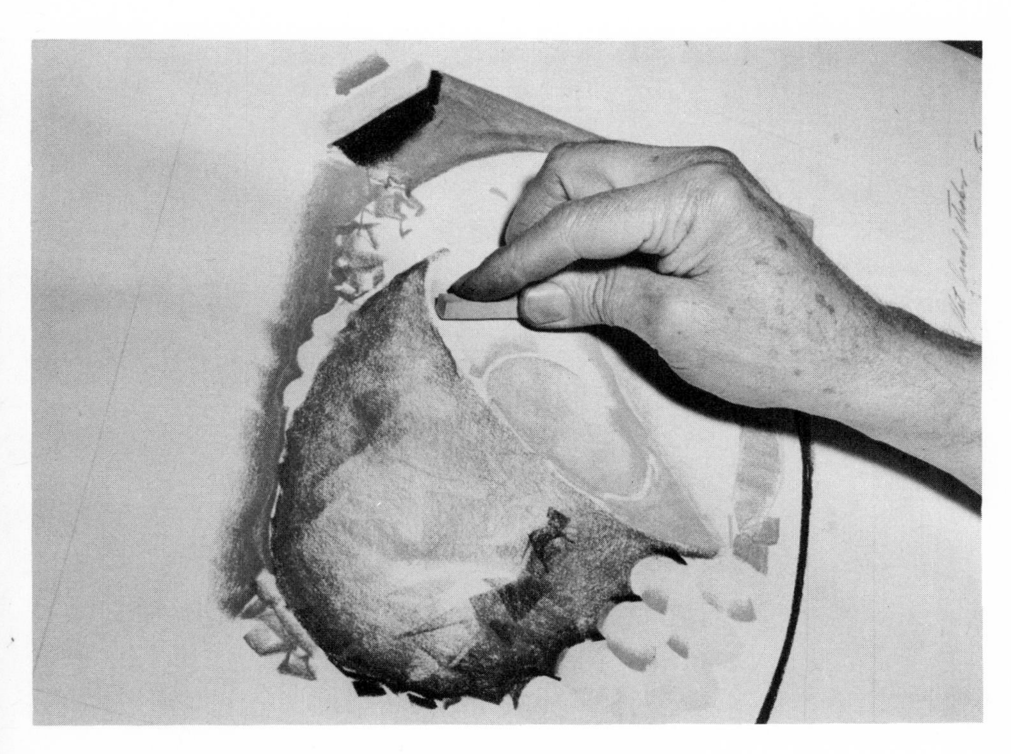

Laying in the pink of the cut ham

Cutting in the blue background

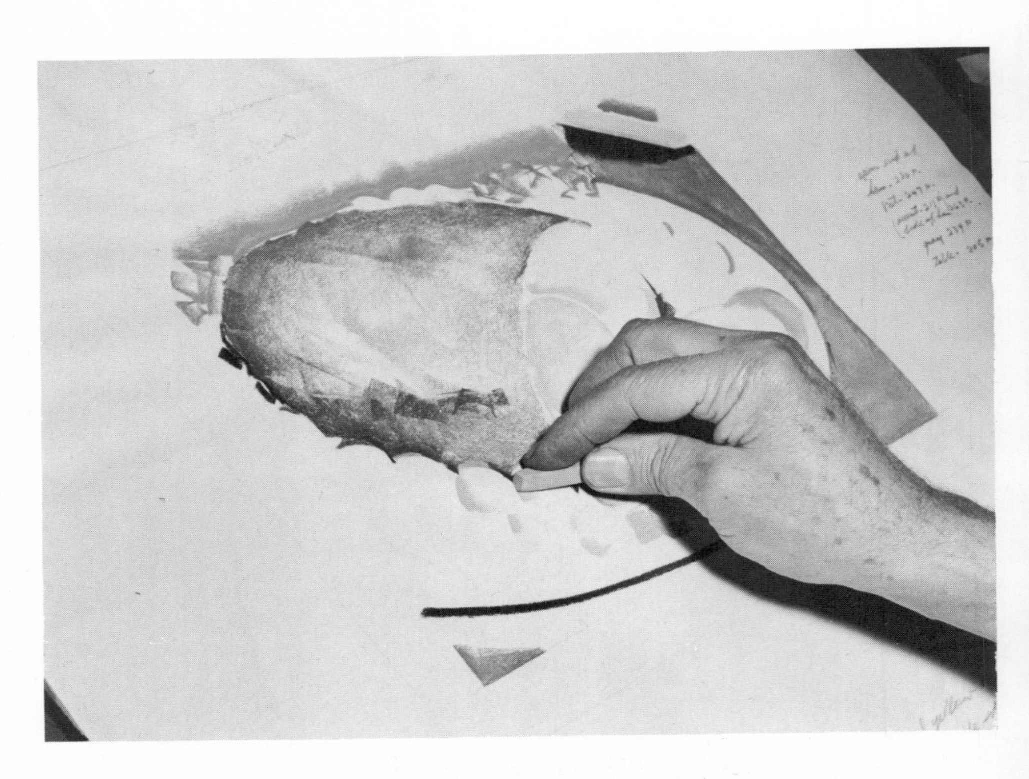

Putting in the shadow on potatoes

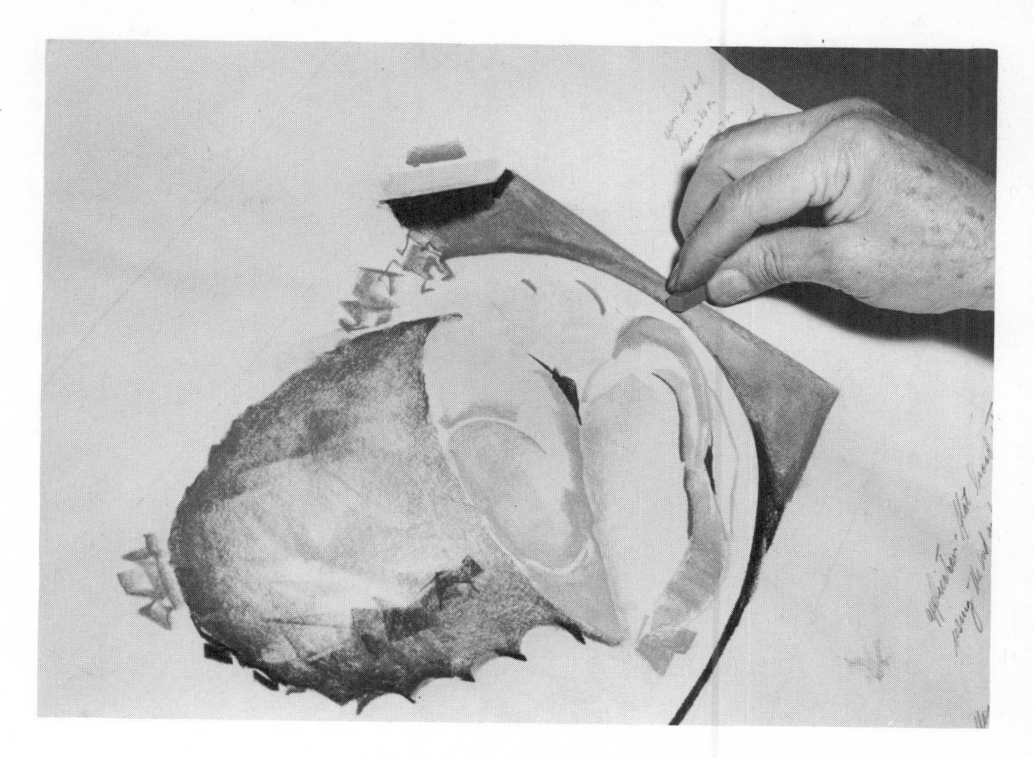

Cutting in edge of plate

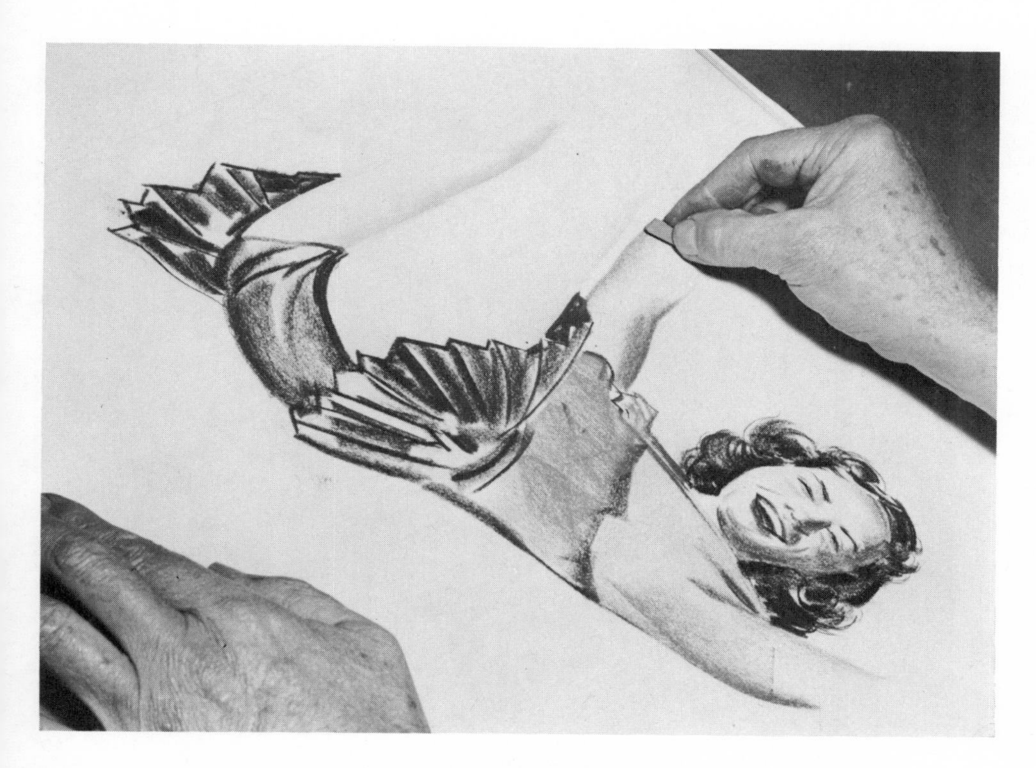

Shadow edge of arm

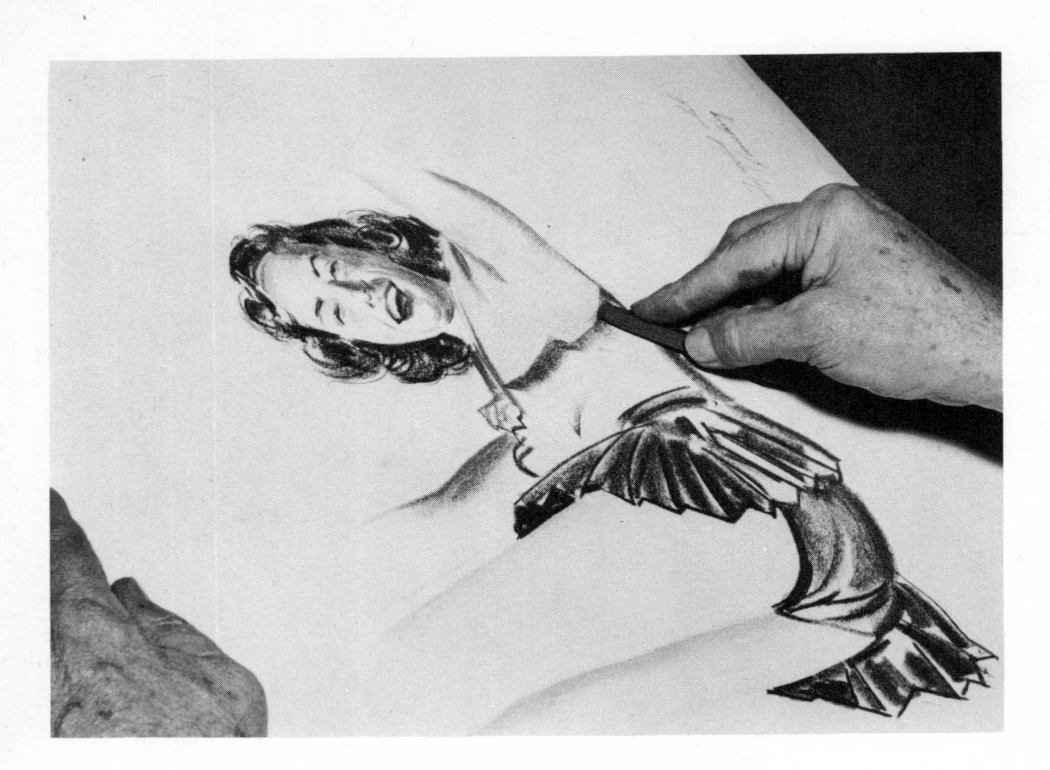

Filling in shadow on body

Paper under hand for protection against smear

How to hold the pastel stick

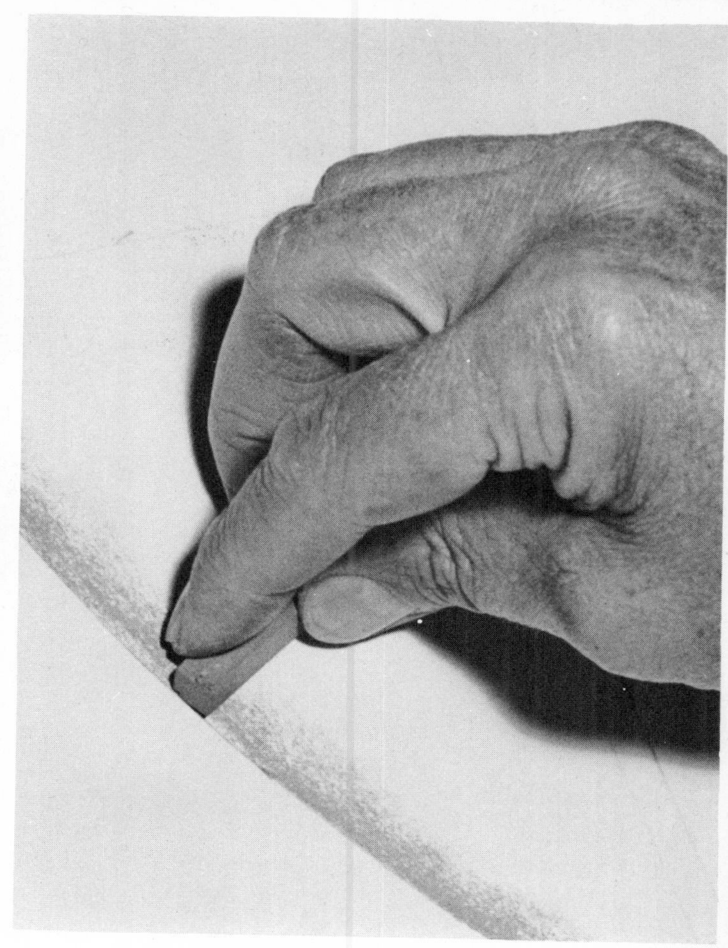

How to apply stick

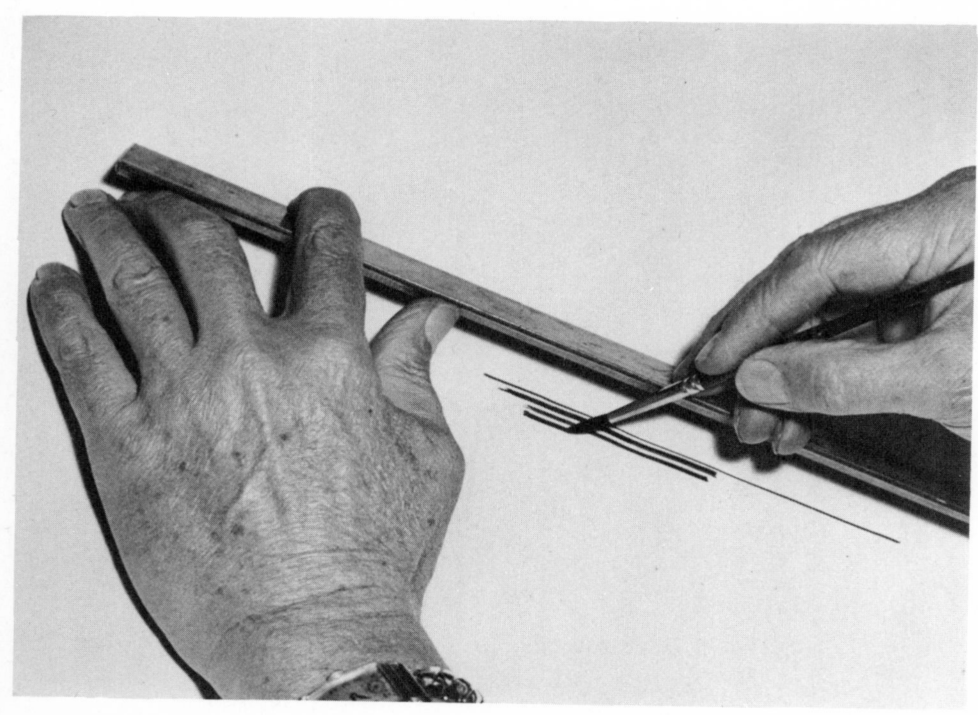

How to line with the brush and ink — note the position of the fingers

GROUP 1
GROUP 2
GROUP 3
1
2
3
GROUP 1
1
2
3
GROUP 2
1
2
3
GROUP 3
3 THIS GROUP FOR LIGHT SIDE OF FACE
2 THIS GROUP FOR SHADOW SIDE OF FACE
1 THIS GROUP FOR HAIR, EYES, MOUTH, AND STRONG ACCENTS

Figures in Action and Three Values

This head has been rendered in flat planes, without any attempt to turn the edges to show the form. Three values are the basic foundation of any painting. Each of these three values has its own family of values, but each family always stays within the big parent value. If the lesser values within a large value are held in the right balance, the art work appears to be composed of three large values.

If you were rendering this same head in black, white, and gray, you would have to resolve them to a very simple arrangement. On the next twelve pages you will find various examples of figures in action with some advice and notes on the importance of value relationship. Any good drawing can turn out a failure if it is rendered with a set of weak values. Strengthen those values and even with a poorly drawn subject it will have a more convincing look. When using color, always think of the *value* rather than the color.

First key drawing

Corrected key drawing

Finished rendering in gray pastel

Actual size of rendering. Three different shades of the gray pastels were used. It is necessary to have the sticks sharpened to a chisel point at one end. To get the broad flat areas, use the square end of the stick. Apply each value in as simple a manner as you can, for in this way you will retain a freshness that cannot be obtained when the pastel is thick in one place and thin in another; evenness of tone is important.

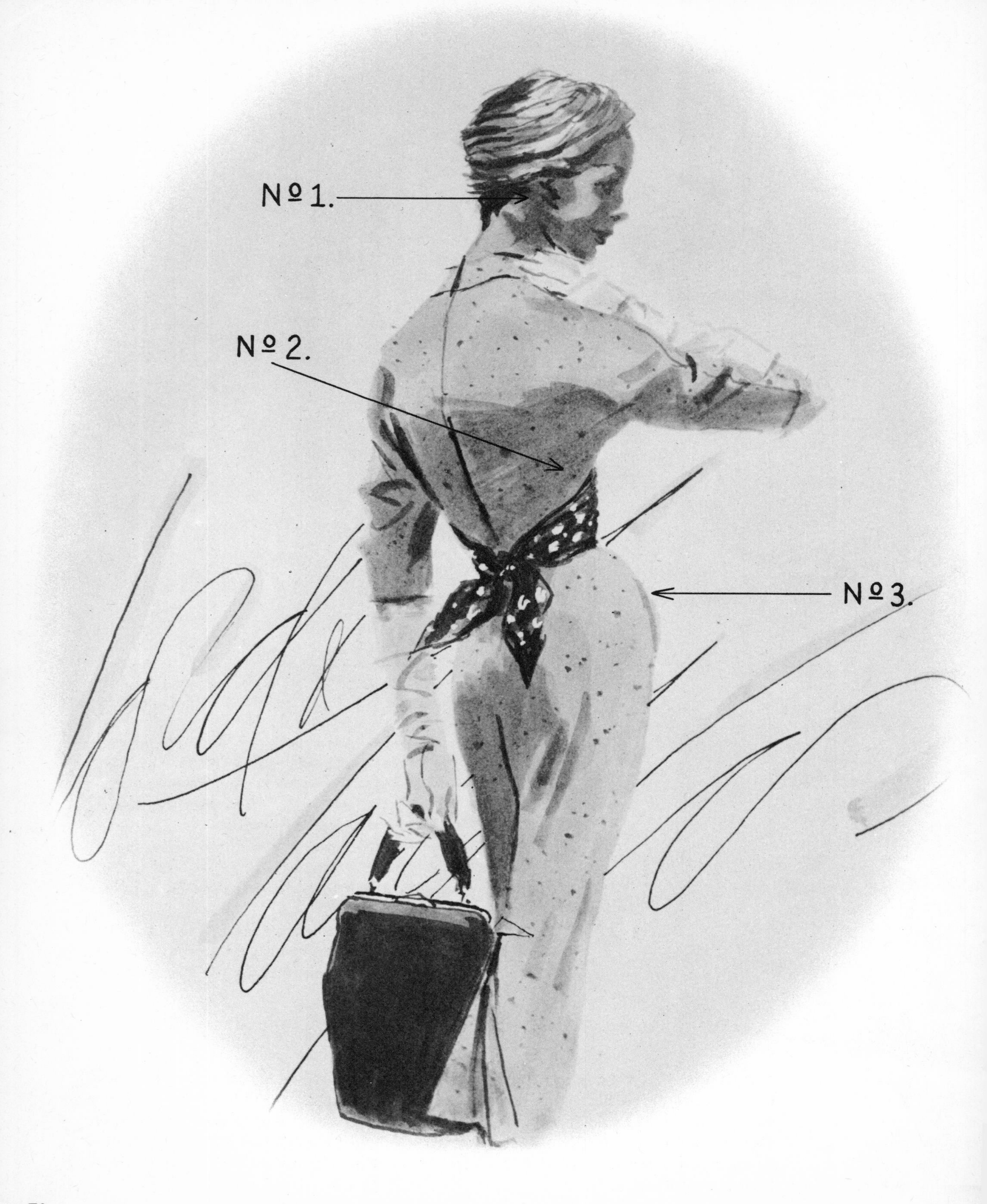
№ 1.
№ 2.
№ 3.

Here are two drawings by Hood for a Lord & Taylor advertisement. Study them carefully and note the simplification of her value relationships and how they work. Notice how simply the shadow of the face has been applied on the girl on the left, leaving the light side of the face and neck in *one* value. The same is true of the shadow area. The back and shoulder area contain *three* values, yet it has the appearance of just *one* value. This applies to the rest of the figure also. The same principles hold true for the girl in the dark dress, where the values are simply darker in tone.

The air of ultra-smartness and sophistication becomes even more forceful and dynamic because the drawings are so bold and simple in their conception of values.

UNSTRETCHED BOND

Graphite and stump

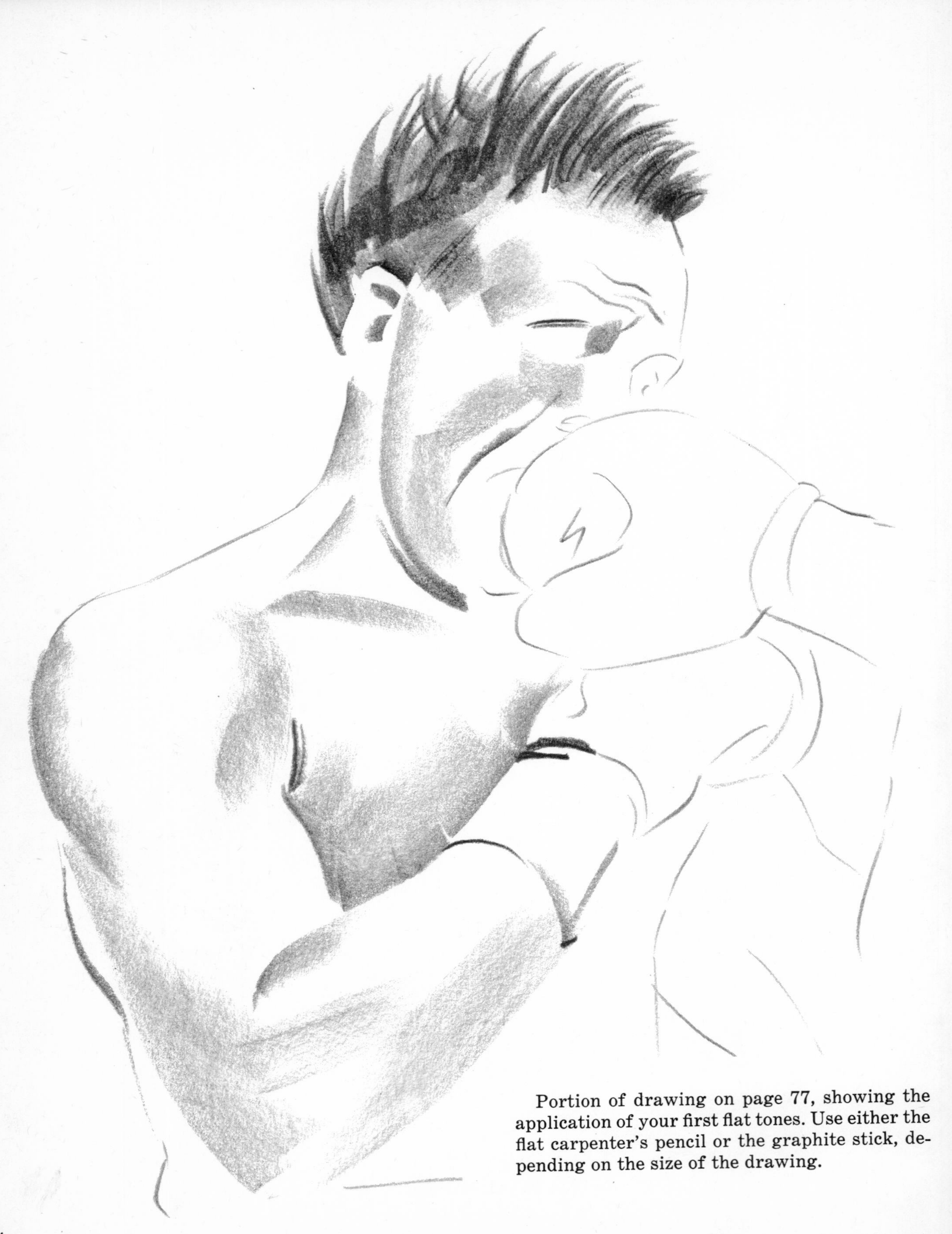

Portion of drawing on page 77, showing the application of your first flat tones. Use either the flat carpenter's pencil or the graphite stick, depending on the size of the drawing.

Wolff pencil, chisel point

Gray chalks, one end sharpened to a chisel point for the fine lines. Use the square end for the flat tones.

A vignette, using a 3-B chisel-point graphite pencil.

Pastel Grays

Here is an interesting example of the various textures one can get by using the chisel point of the gray chalks. Apply the larger flat values with the side of the stick. For the final sharp detail use the Wolff pencil too. The whites must be retained by cutting in with the corner of the square end of the stick.

Cado (Flo-Master) Pen

On the next five pages are examples of various subjects rendered with the Cado (Flo-Master) pen. As with all other mediums, you must get acquainted with it before you can hope to get the most out of it. The varied types of points available make it a flexible medium for both tone and line. It comes in black and colored inks. It is tricky to use and is one medium that requires a great deal of practice to master.

This is a good medium to use as an underlay for a finished comprehensive; it will show through the bond paper more clearly than pencil.

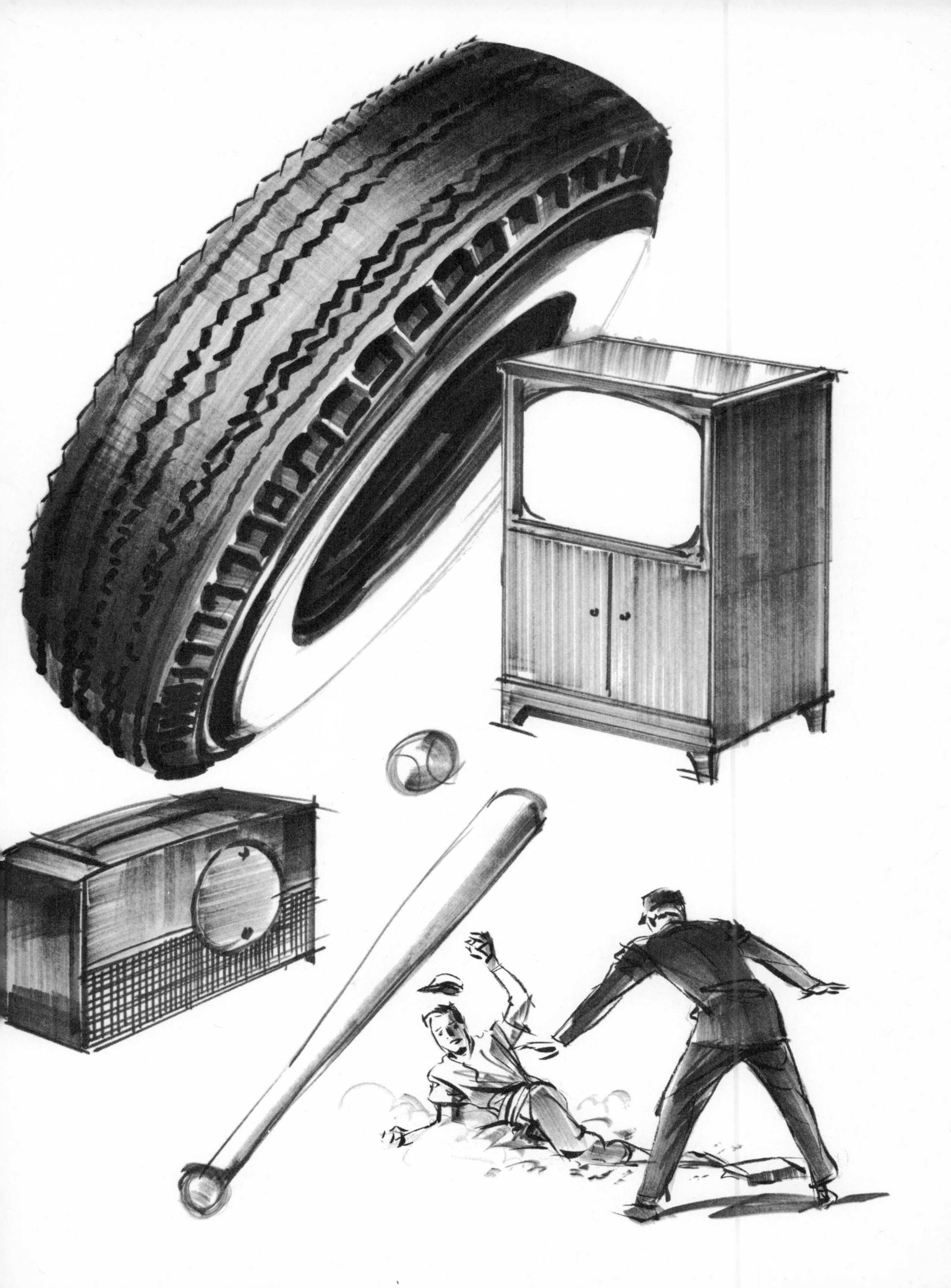

NAVY
10

Scrap

Your reference file is very important. If you have not started one, do so. Some of the listings should be as follows: girls, men, houses, animals, industrial, horses, interiors. Clip magazines and news photos for your own reference. The example on page 87 was rendered from a baseball news shot. You will find that a file of newspaper shots or any other source of tear sheets is most valuable when you tackle a job. You will have a file of action that you could not duplicate, even if you had the models and the photographic equipment to take the photos yourself. The more complete your file is, the better your rendering will be.

Key drawings using
newspaper scrap

Simple Pencil Renderings

BRUSH AND INK-
THREE VALUES

Animals in Action

The drawings of the dogs on the facing page were made with brush and ink, using a No. 3 red sable brush for the first step in establishing the lines. Then the second value was applied, let dry, and the third value applied. In each case, simplicity was the by-word. The dog at the bottom right is missing the middle value, and yet it still carries as a unit. I cannot stress too much the importance of these three major values in any rendering, as they are always the heart of any well organized drawing.

This is the key drawing for the rendering on page 93.

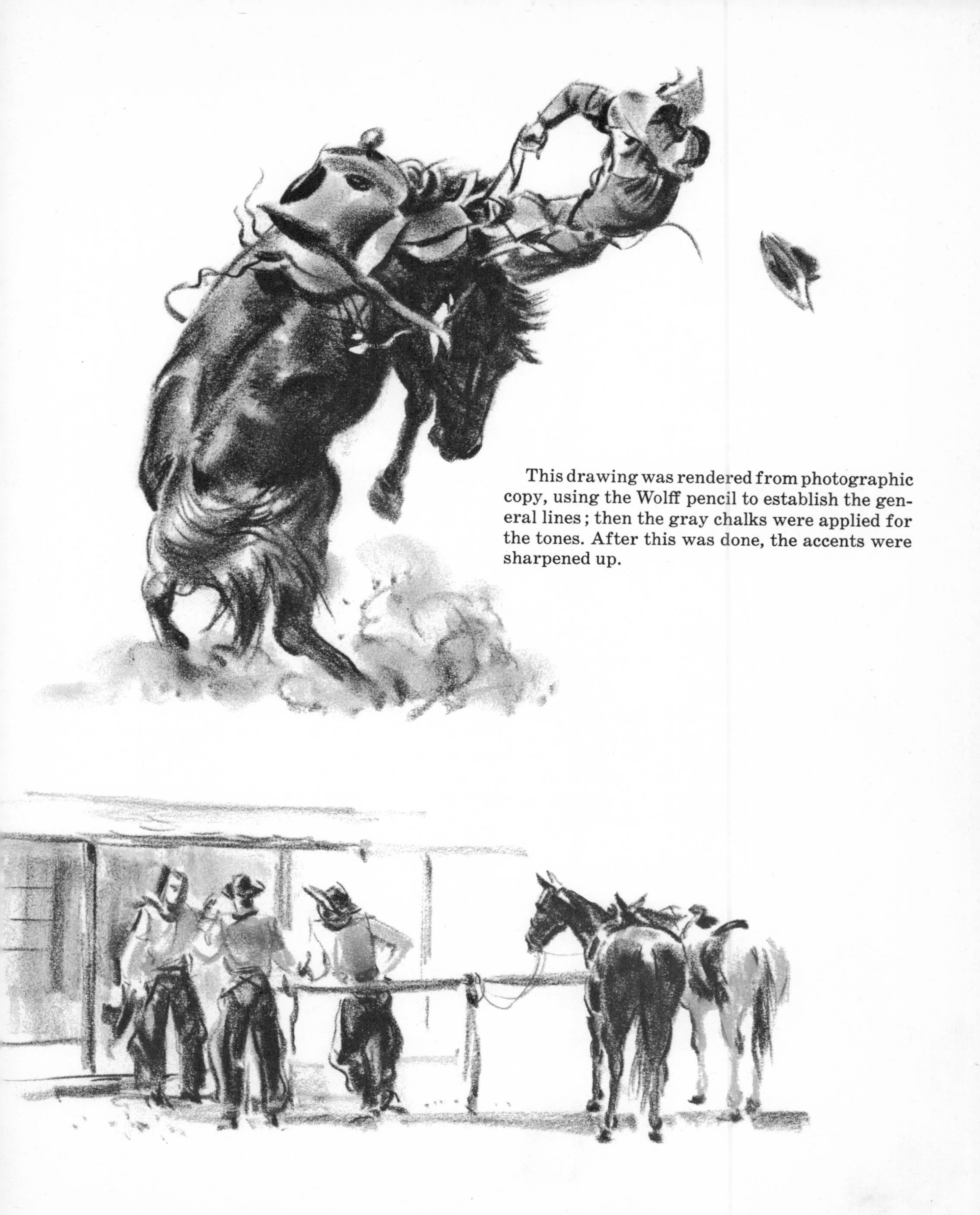

This drawing was rendered from photographic copy, using the Wolff pencil to establish the general lines; then the gray chalks were applied for the tones. After this was done, the accents were sharpened up.

Textures

Used in conjunction with the rendering of clothing, furniture coverings, etc. By placing any one of several types of board under your sheet of layout paper, then applying your pencil on the portion where you want the texture to show, an interesting texture can be accomplished very quickly. Try experimenting with all kinds of rough board to see the unusual effects you can get. On pages 95, 96, and 97 are several examples. The graphite stick is best to use for the average area.

Corrugated board under layout for texture. Charcoal pencil for line.

Ink and brush for the line, using a piece of Masonite for texture under a sheet of bond paper.

1 Masonite

2 Flat graphite stick

3 Mat board

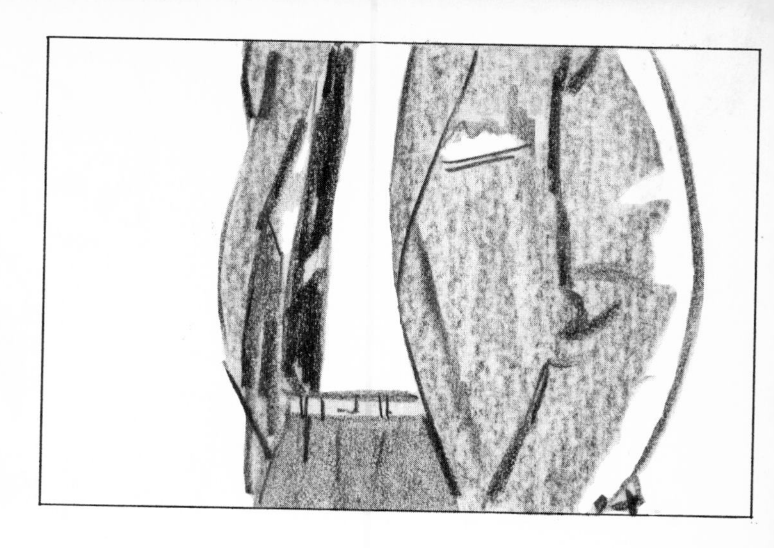

4 Rough cardboard

5 Masonite

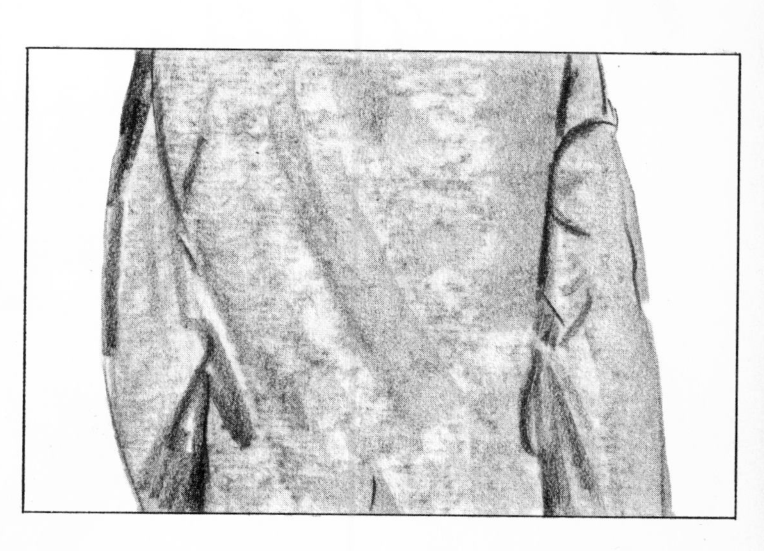

6 Back of layout pad

Color Pastels

You have been introduced to the various mediums and the tools that are to be used, now let's try out the color pastels. Here is a rather simple problem for you to render.

First make a careful key drawing and place it under a fresh sheet of bond paper. Never work with pastel when your layout pad has only a few sheets of paper left on it. Take a full pad and tape your key drawing on it, then put the fresh sheet of paper on top of that. Otherwise, your pastel is likely to show streaks.

First, with the flat side of the stick and using the corner edge, lay in the pink No. 246-P lightly. Then with the flat edge, stroke in the secondary half tones of the dress. The light tones of the flesh are made with No. 276-P, with a light overtone of No. 207-P for the reflected light. For the dark accents and shadow side of the arm use No. 213-P and for the hair use No. 263-P. Use gray chalk on the shoes with a light touch of No. 233-P on the heels. Use the lightest gray in the set of gray pastels for the shadow on the white panties. By using the sharpened chisel point of the pastel, you will be able to get those sharp accents that make your rendering look crisp.

When fixing any pastel, first clean all white areas with kneaded eraser squeezed to the desired shape to get into small places. After this is done and the loose color has been blown off, hold the fix can directly above the rendering and spray it lightly. Let it dry a few seconds, then fix it again.

FOOTBALL
COLD?
SKIING
SNOWMEN
SKATING
SHOVELING
SLEDDING
Once a day... every day... SOUP!

This is a Soup Pitcher
Once a day... every day... SOUP!

How to Make Rendering Pay Off

By Harold Olsen

Art Director at Batten, Barton, Durstine & Osborn, Inc.

Anyone in commercial art can do better rendering and make it more profitable if he recognizes the fact that he is a *commercial* artist.

The basic difference between "fine art" and "commercial art" is that the former is the expression of the feelings and interests of an individual *without* regard for the opinions of others, whereas the latter subordinates the ego of the individual *in favor* of influencing the interests of others.

All successful art directors, illustrators, photographers, designers, cartoonists, or other specialists in the graphic arts that I've ever met, recognize that they are "pictorial salesmen." They have one common starting point, whether they're selling cars or bras, food or fashions, liquor or lingerie, charity or cigarettes: They realize they have to sell a specific product or idea to a particular group of customers, simply, clearly, and persuasively by *visual* means.

Here are some of the basic questions they ask *before* they start rendering a job. It makes good sense to follow the method of "men who know commercial art best."

1. What am I trying to sell?
2. Whom am I trying to sell it to?
3. What are these particular people interested in?
4. Where will the advertising appear?
5. How can the approach be made pertinent to the product?
6. What is the basic character of the product or advertising approach?
7. What subject matter will appeal to most of the customers?
8. How can this subject matter be made more interesting?
9. What is the basic idea of the advertisement?
10. How simply and quickly can the idea be presented?
11. Is this advertisement part of a series?
12. What design principles can best organize and dramatize these ideas pictorially?

The time you save in organizing your thinking by following this method will give you the chance to consider the "extras" that make your work distinctive and compelling. "Extras" such as the right types of people, wearing the correct clothing, hair styles, and accessories, in surroundings with the right background to compliment them — in other words, "good casting"; careful consideration of the proper mood and of the gestures and attitudes of the subjects, so that everything is in harmony with the appeal; and, finally, the inspirational "extras" that you get from an awareness of the world around you, to keep your work fresh and contemporary. All these "extras" can't help but improve your rendering.

One last bit of advice: keep your renderings broad and simple; avoid noodling. More renderings have been ruined by too much time than by too little.

This orderly, positive approach has proven successful in the past for many people in commercial art — and could be the same for you.

Bob Bode

Art Director at Kudner Agency, Inc.

WITH INDUSTRIAL SUBJECTS, AN ATTEMPT IS MADE TO CREATE DRAMATIC FEELING THROUGH ESTABLISHING INTERESTING COLOR AND VALUE PATTERNS. BOTH BEING APPLIED SPONTANEOUSLY AND SIMPLY

TWO COLOR AVIATION SKETCH.. BASIC BLACK AND WHITE DRAWING DONE WITH FELT TIP LAYOUT PEN AND INDIA INK LINE· WATER COLOR WASH PLUS PASTEL CHALK FOR TEXTURES

DETAIL UNNECESSARY WHEN PATTERN AND COLOR VAL WORK TOGETHE SOMETIMES HEL FOR VIEWER TO READ OWN IMPRESSIONS IN A ROUGH.

WATER COLOR SKETCH WITH NO ATTEMPT AT DETAIL. SINCE EFFECT AND MOOD SEEM TO BE ESTABLISHED, NO AMOUNT OF ADDED DETAIL WOULD HELP PICTURE.

AN ATTEMPT TO PAINT WITH LINE CAN BE VERY EFFECTIVE IF LINE IS SENSITIVE AND PATTERN DRAMATIC.

Charles Hawes

Sketch Artist at Lennen & Newell, Inc.

The creative operation of an agency today demands of a sketch man clarity without sacrifice of time. Such pace and clarity is achieved by sound underlying draftsmanship (proportion, action, and composition) combined with an absolute minimum of values and details. This does not mean, however, that all sketches may appear flat and formulated. It is the sketch man's responsibility to capture the spirit of the idea to be conveyed to the client. For example, in the sketches reproduced on these pages we have two different subjects handled emotionally in the manner each idea demanded. For the American Airlines advertisement a sketch was prepared showing well-groomed passengers disembarking after a flight and obviously well pleased with the airline's service. In the second sketch, the emotional appeal of young children dashing out to fill a picnic basket with beans called for a broader dramatic approach bordering on the cartoon. Two different emotions, yes, but both were achieved with the same principle of rendering . . . sound draftsmanship, a minimum of values, and a minimum of details.

Advice to the Young Artist

In the commercial field, whether you free-lance or are employed in an art studio or advertising agency, you will come into eventual contact with the art director. The art director is the man who works with the client and the account executive, putting all the elements of the advertisement together.

It is up to you to try to please the art director in his particular problem — the pictorial part of an advertisement. Sometimes an art director will give you just a few penciled indications on paper, within the area in which you are to render a picture. Then again, you may get a very nicely stated, if rough, indication of what is wanted. The latter makes it much easier for you to tackle the job, eliminating the guesswork on your part. The next step is to assemble any scrap or reference you may need. Don't be hasty in starting — familiarize yourself first with all the elements that must be embodied in the illustration.

Many art directors are so involved with details that they do not have time to render a comp or get all the information you may need. From the very beginning, form the habit of always doing the best job you can within the alloted time. You will find it pays off in the end. Above all, don't be afraid to ask for help from the "pros" about you. You will find them ready to give you the help you need. In the beginning many a job of mine was saved by fellow artists with just a few deft strokes, and I have been more than happy to return that favor to other beginners. Remember, all artists started at the point you'll be at when you begin, and they will be more than understanding and glad to help you.

Always be well versed on all the subjects you will be called on to do. Constantly practice all the mediums, sketch outside whenever you find a spare moment. Acquire a first-hand knowledge of many handlings, digest them, and learn to inject them into a commercial interpretation. The better "fine" artist you are, the better rendered job you will be able to do.

If a young artist constantly experiments with different mediums, he's on the right track, but the success of mastering any one of them is built upon a large stack of failures — *so start stacking!*

On page 107 is the final rendering for a shirt ad, rendered by using a palette knife and casein color on black cardboard.

About Color

A sense of color, if you have it, is a most valuable asset. You will find this so as you move from black and white to color pastels. Always think of the *value* rather than the color of the subject matter at hand. It is the *value* of red, blue, or yellow that counts, not just the color red, blue, or yellow. If you have a red automobile to do, of course, it must be a certain color of red, either warm or cool, but the value of the color is of prime importance. You must keep the areas as simple as possible. In both the light and the dark portions, the natural tendency is to over-model. This kind of a rendering always looks labored; it is better to have too little than too much detail. Remember that when you fill the tooth of the paper with pastel, anything more added will not remain the same after fixing. The color underneath will come through, so try to merge the tones or colors into each other while there is still tooth on the paper to receive it. You will find that colors will merge together with a light rub of the finger tip.

In transparent watercolor, the rule is somewhat the same. Cover the large areas with a wide stroke quickly. Then, while the surface is still wet, introduce a varied color or different value within it and have it retain its unit strength. Above all, experiment with all your mediums constantly. The sooner you become acquainted with them and how they work, the sooner your renderings will improve.

Cat Cracker

This is the comprehensive rendered in wash watercolors. The fine lines of white were put on in opaque after the larger units were completed.

Here is the pencil rough used in rendering the comprehensive. The color comprehensive was rendered in wash. The fine lines were put on with opaque white. On page 124 is the finished art work, also done in wash.

An Ad Is Born

A four-step process:
Step 1. The art director, the account man, and the client get together at a meeting and decide what they want and how to say it in an ad. This is generally the conversation stage.
Step 2. The art director then takes his notes, either mental or written, and goes to his board and starts to work. He organizes all the elements desired in the ad, usually working very quickly and roughly.
Step 3. Then the art director calls in the artist who is to do the rendering. They discuss the over-all problem. Then the artist is given a photograph of the car in the exact position. He

then proceeds to do any research on other elements that are needed in the ad before he starts making his comprehensive.

Step 4. If the final presentation is approved, and the finish is to be a photograph, the art director then has to arrange for the photographer, the models, and the location. In this case the theme of the ad was yellow — so Florida was chosen for these shots. In all cases, the art director, the models, the correct clothes, and the photographer take off for the location. Of course, sometimes the weather does not cooperate and the entire crew must wait for sunshine and the right time of day. Many, many shots are taken, but usually only one of these will be used. After the selection of the photograph, the photographer goes to work on the final print. This in turn goes to the art director for approval and to the client. When it has been approved all around, it goes to the engraver and then is ready for the press.

Boat Yard

Here is an example of simplified values. Notice how little you have to do to say so much. If you analyze each unit, you will find I have used two and sometimes three values. By doing this, I retained the impact of the large areas — nothing is broken up into small units — giving a more convincing picture.

Whenever you are trying to show sunlight, remember that white is as high as anyone can go in value — so retain the white of the paper for that purpose. Do not share the mistaken belief that yellow is sunlight. There may be a yellow object in sunlight that will take on a very light tone of yellow, but the light itself is not yellow. Note, also, how sparingly the dark accents have been used. These are the values that oppose the halftones and the light areas, yet complement each other.

This is the key drawing used in the pastel rendering "Boat Yard," reproduced in color on the two following pages.

Girl in Black Sweater

Although the finish was rendered in casein, you will find that you can approximate the finished painting by using pastels. Follow the number of the pastels noted by the side of the drawing on page 120. This is a fast medium to use once you become acquainted with it. You will also find that once it is fixed you can use an opaque paint to make corrections or add detail to the drawing.

Pencil drawing used as the key for pastel rendering on page 120.

Pastel rendering, unfinished, so that you may see just how it is approached.

This is the finished art work, rendered in casein, a medium similar to opaque or designer's colors but one that will not blend with water after it has dried.

Drawing by John Dunn

Art Director at Batten, Barton, Durstine & Osborn, Inc.

Storyboards

Each new medium in advertising is a new challenge — how best to present it to the public and how to satisfy the client's needs and desires. The advent of television brought such a problem. The art departments of the larger agencies went to work on this new problem. To tell the story of a particular product, they devised a way of making drawings, in sequence, wtihin the shape of a TV screen on a layout pad. This method is used by the producer of the commercial as a guide to follow in preparing the film for future use on each program. These drawings are rendered in many mediums — wash, pencil, Cado pen, and inks. They are often made over many times until the desired results have been achieved and okayed by the client. Below is an article by Mr. Larry Berger explaining the details of this medium, accompanied by illustrative examples.

Television Art Direction

by Lawrence Berger

Art Director at Batten, Barton, Durstine & Osborn, Inc.

The television commercial is the newest form of advertising to come down the pike. It creates opportunities and presents limitations to test the mettle of any artist. It also demands more specialists than any other media. They include: scenic designers, fashion experts, animators, cartoonists, display designers, set decorators, layout men, and art directors.

The TV art director is many times the key man in conceiving the idea behind the TV spot. The term TV art director is really used more as a convenience than a description. Since the duties of his job are so diverse and may enter into fields remotely associated with actual art supervision, it is not a completely satisfactory term. However, until a better one comes along, TV art director it is.

Many of our TV art experts come with a background of ad agency experience. In fact, those agencies that do a large television volume usually encourage artists from "print" to go into TV. There is no substitute for the experience gained in planning ads when tackling a TV problem. At this point, it may be interesting to compare the TV art director with his counterpart in printed media.

Just as the "print" art director must accumulate a wide knowledge of production knowhow, the TV art director must also saturate himself with as much technical knowledge as is possible. His gamut runs from live to film techniques and incorporates the multitudinous processes that go into TV transmission. Without this knowledge, the handicaps presented may be insurmountable.

Another comparison lies in the difference in structure between the two mediums. An ad is governed by the size of the publication. A spot commercial is limited by the rigid demands of time. Added to this is perhaps the greatest difference: the advantage of movement that TV offers. Consequently, the ad and the commercial may use the same ingredients to tell the story, but the forms they take are completely different.

For example, the same type face and product illustration might be used in both mediums, but in TV the lettering most likely would be an optical effect or transition from one scene to another. The same holds true for the package or product. That, too, might move forward, zoom back, or twist and turn,

This is the finished art work, rendered in wash. The actual size is 20 inches high and 12 inches wide. See pages 109 and 110 for the preliminary stages.

wiping on still other effects, important phrases, or new scenes. The judicious use of these effects can add impact to a commercial; used indiscriminately, they can make the spot irritating.

Most people in the field of advertising are quite familiar with the duties of the "print" art director, but the TV art director is still a man from Mars. What is his role? We have mentioned that he may be the key man behind the conception of an idea. It is his duty to lay out the storyboard, supervise the styling of the commercial, suggest settings, decide upon the type of animation if that is called for, help choose the production outfit, and approve all the artwork. In addition, he attends recording sessions, film shootings, and follows through till the job is completed.

The TV art director's layout pad is the storyboard. The storyboard is simply a series of drawings or photographs with a panel below each picture that describes the action known as "video" and the spoken copy and sound effects, referred to as "audio."

These panels form the continuity of a proposed commercial, giving as complete a picture of the finished product as is possible at this stage. In addition, the storyboard is the blueprint for production and the means of presentation to the client. It is of great importance that the rendering of the storyboard frames fit the action of the commercial, rather than form a string of unrelated pictures. The techniques utilized in illustrating the individual panels are a matter of degree based on the type of presentation to be made. The techniques may vary, but good drawing is as basic to TV as it is to all other forms of graphic presentation. The actual drawings that make up the storyboard may be wash, charcoal, pencil, or pastel. The artists rendering the panels must visualize background, setting, movements of actors or products, lettering, optical effects, lighting, package display, and whatever else is to be shown. He must be able to translate video directions in terms of the camera view finder, and his drawings must guide the producer who will follow the storyboard.

One of the more interesting forms of commercial is the animated cartoon. An animated spot accompanies a product that calls for a "lighter sell" technique, but that does not mean animation is used only for entertainment. Rather it is called upon when it will do a better selling job than any other technique.

The art director must be vigilant because mistakes in animated films are costly. Once the animated spot goes into production, the art director is always in contact with the animators. He checks all art work — character styling, background, color, product, and pencil tests for flow of action and composition. In addition, he checks the film quality, synchronization of music, voice, and picture, and maintains constant check on production schedules.

Animation seems to be a creature of trends. It is simple for animated spots to fall into the trap of current vogues — which ultimately shows up on the screen as third-rate copies of what was an original idea. In the hands of creative artists the styling of an animated spot can be a stimulating experience, whether the form used is realism, stylization, or abstraction. Applying a current popular style of animation to every product just because it was successful for a competitive product is academic and can look woefully unoriginal. Successful commercials should apply the current technique to the specific product. It must take into consideration the tone of the commercial, who it is directed at, and how the product is used.

There is much left unsaid about the many problems of TV transmission and how they affect finished artwork. The importance of artwork preparation for transmission is a large field and would call for another article. The advent of color TV and the transmission of black and white from color artwork requires an entirely new approach toward color design. The human eye used to be the sole judge of good color values. It now must share that spot with the electronic eye which resolves color into tones of gray. Therefore, the color artwork must be adjusted to fit both color and black and white transmission facilities. The problem of where good taste ends and expediency begins is the challenge of the TV art director.

VIDEO: MARCH ON SET.

AUDIO: MARCH (ON)

[illegible] ...the biggest, most glamorous beauty [illegible] of the year... [illegible]

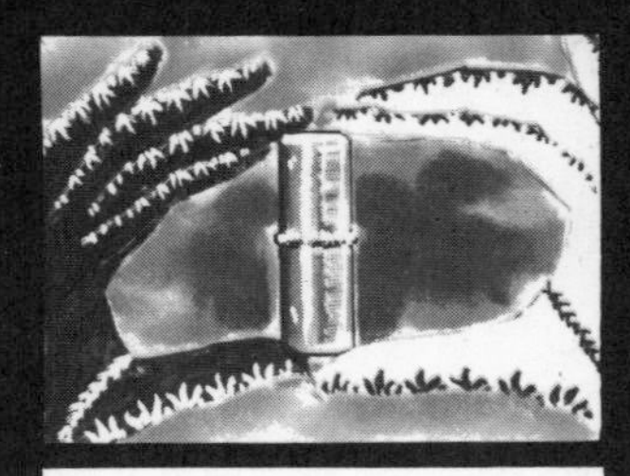

VIDEO: CUT TO HANDS IN GLAMOROUS GLOVES HOLDING UP FUTURAMA.

AUDIO: CHORUS (OVER)

The Fabulous...

VIDEO: CUT TO HANDS IN OUTRAGEOUSLY CHIC GLOVES HOLDING UP FUTURAMA.

AUDIO: Fabulous...

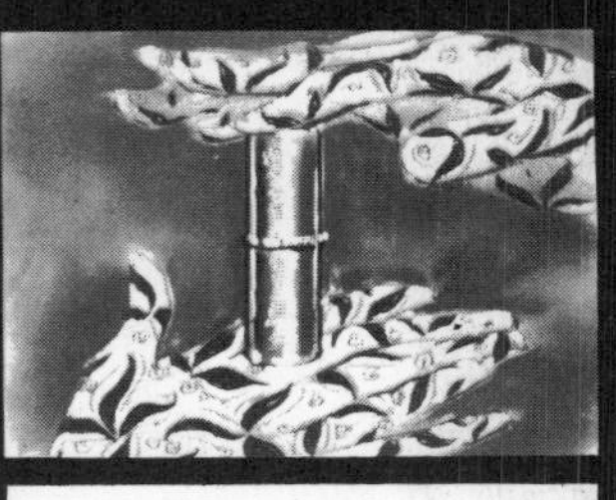

VIDEO: CUT TO HANDS IN REAL EXCITING GLOVES HOLDING UP FUTURAMA.

AUDIO: Fabulous...

VIDEO: IN TO TOP OF FUTURAMA.

AUDIO: Futurama...for you...

VIDEO: FROM THE FUTURAMA PULL BACK TO PATRICK HOLDING UP FUTURAMA. PATRICK IS WEARING MAGNIFICENT GOLD-LOOKING EVENING GOWN.

AUDIO: PATRICK (ON)

(FABULOUS FUTURAMA MUSIC UNDER)

Fabulously beautiful...designed by Van Cleef and Arpels... jewelers to the best dressed women in the world!

VIDEO: SHE TAKES OFF CAP, SWIVELS UP LIPSTICK, GESTURES AS IF ABOUT TO PUT ON LIPSTICK. RECAPS CASE.

AUDIO: Fabulously chic....this gleaming brushed gold Futurama gives an elegant jewelry touch to any costume you wear...makes even the gesture of putting on lipstick a thing of beauty...Now you might think a magnificent case like this would cost a king's ransom.. but get set for a shock (music ping)
(MUSIC STOPS)

VIDEO: CUT TO CU GLAMOR SHOT OF CASE WITH CAP LAYING BESIDE...LIPSTICK SWIVELED UP...PAT ON "ONLY $1.25"

AUDIO: PATRICK (OVER)

This exquisite Futurama is yours...complete with your favorite Revlon lipstick...for only $1.25...imagine...only $1.25...the price you'd pay for lipstick in any ordinary case!

VIDEO: CUT TO PATRICK.

AUDIO: PATRICK (ON)

[illegible]...and your beautiful Futurama saves you money day after day...year after year because

VIDEO: PAT "PERMANENT CASE"

AUDIO: PATRICK (ON)

Your Futurama is a permanent case. That means you no longer have to pay for an old fashioned brass case each time you need a new lipstick...

VIDEO: SAVE 35¢ ON EACH LIPSTICK.

AUDIO: PATRICK (ON)

Simply buy a Revlon refill for your permanent Futurama and you save 35¢ every time. You see, Revlon refills are regular lipstick-sized and cost just 90¢

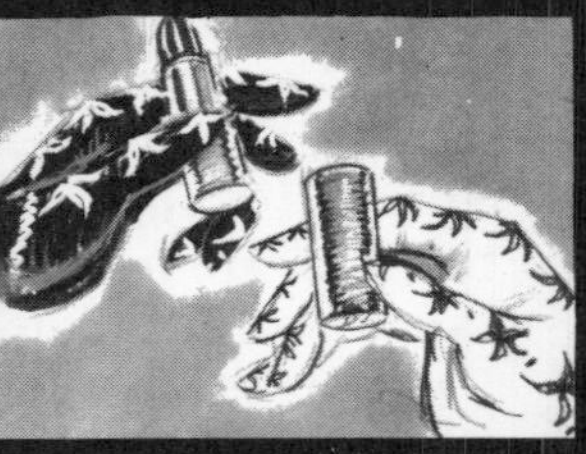

VIDEO: MODEL WEARING GLOVES HAND DEMONSTRATES ... CLICKS OUT ONE.

AUDIO: And it's so quick, so convenient to change the refills! Just click out yesterday's shade ...

VIDEO: SHE PUTS IN ANOTHER...[illegible] RECAPS FUTURAMA.

AUDIO: ... click in the shade you want today! Your fingers can't get messy because your lipstick never touches them!

VIDEO: CUT TO DISPLAY OF CASE WITH CAP ON...NEXT TO IT 3 LIPSTICKS (OPEN) TO DESIGNATE THE 3 TYPES OF LIPSTICK. HAND PUTS THEM IN SYNC WITH AUDIO.

AUDIO: PATRICK (OVER)

And the beauty of it is you have your choice of Futurama refills in any of Revlon's 28 radiant shades...any of Revlon's three famous lipstick types...[illegible]...lustrous or Revlon Living...

VIDEO: CUT TO PATRICK

AUDIO: PATRICK (ON)

(MUSIC UNDER) So girls...glamorize your lips and your costume with...

VIDEO: REVOLVING GLAMOR DISPLAY OF FUTURAMA.

AUDIO: CHORUS (OVER)

Fabulous....Futurama....For you...

VIDEO: MARCH [illegible]

AUDIO: MARCH (ON)

[illegible] Revlon's new Gold-tone Futurama ... [illegible] $1.25. Get yours tomorrow!

An example of a live action storyboard rendered for Revlon Products. The technique shown is excellent for style and clarity. Gray chalks were used.

This is a ten second station I.D. combining live action and animation for Schaefer Beer. The slogan "for real enjoyment" (panel 1) animated into the glass of beer (panel 2).

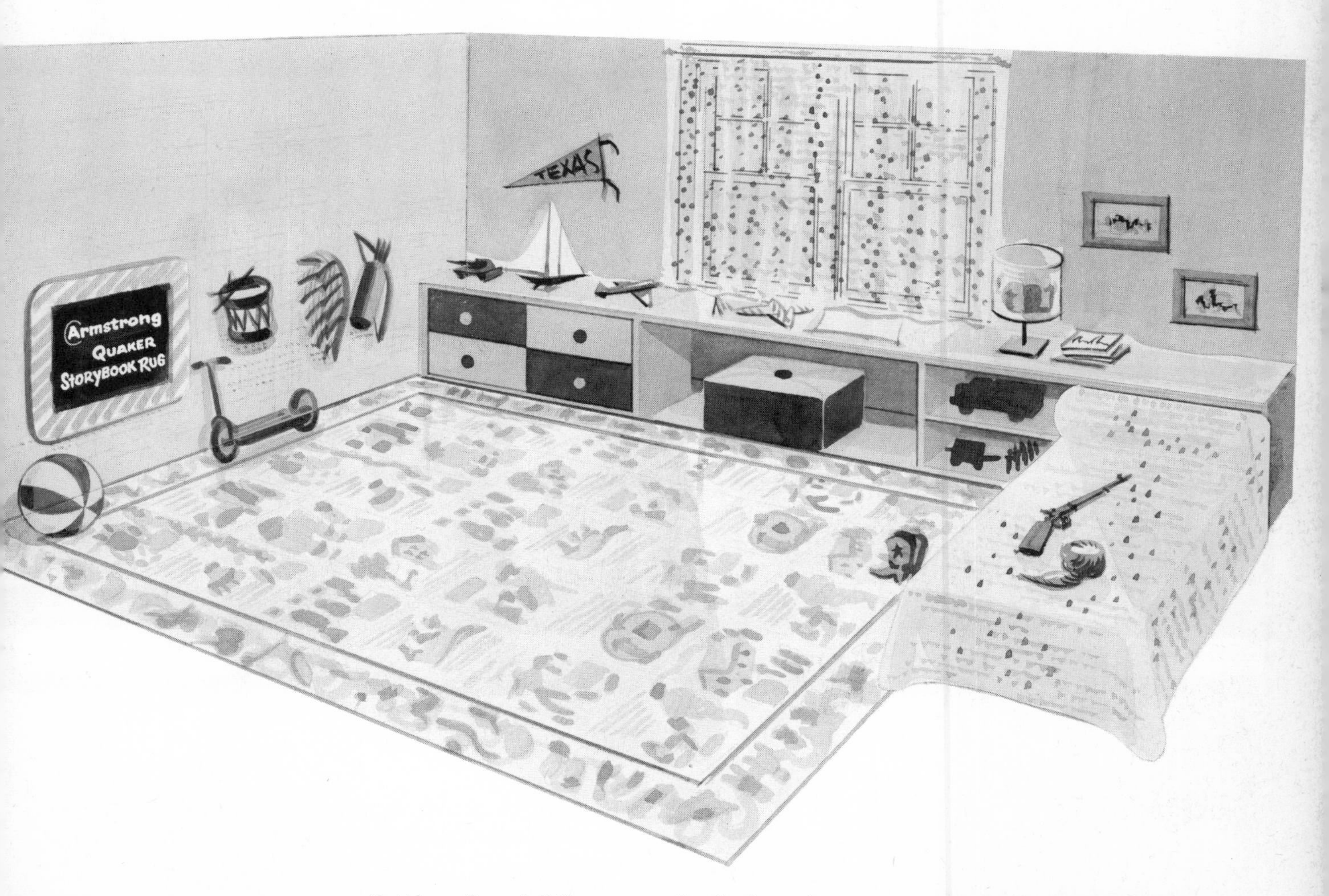

Setting for child's room displaying Armstrong Quaker "Storybook Rug" in a live commercial. This set became the focal point for the commercial.

Storyboard rendering for General Mills displaying the use of "sampler" type animation. This storyboard also indicates live action inserts.

VIDEO: PAN OVER TO SHOW SAMPLER FLOWERS ON WINDOW SILL.
AUDIO: and flowers grow on window sills
VIDEO: CUT TO CU SAMPLER WOMAN TAKING CAKE IN PAN OUT OF OVEN.
AUDIO: ... you can bake a higher cake
Betty Crocker
Angel Food
VIDEO: CUT TO CU SAMPLER WOMAN PICKING UP CAKE IN PAN AND DANCING AROUND ...
AUDIO: ... a lighter cake
Betty Crocker
Angel Food
VIDEO: SHE MAKES COMPLETE TURN ... REVEALS CAKE IN PAN HAS CHANGED TO CAKE ON PLATTER.
AUDIO: ... a better-tasting cake than any you've ever known.
Betty Crocker
Angel Food
VIDEO: SAMPLER WOMAN WALKS BACK INTO ORIGINAL SAMPLER ... PLACING PACKAGE ON TABLE.
AUDIO: You have Betty Crocker's promise of a perfect cake ...
A perfect Cake
Every Time
Betty Crocker
Angel Food
VIDEO: PULL BACK FROM SAMPLER REVEALING ANGEL FOOD CAKE AND PACKAGE ON TABLE IN FRONT OF SAMPLER. LEGEND ON SAMPLER QUICKLY RESTITCHES ITSELF TO READ:
A PERFECT CAKE EVERY TIME
AUDIO: Angel perfect — every time you bake

Ten Top-Flight Artists

On the next 20 pages are examples of the work of ten top-flight artists who are producing finished art as well as comprehensives every day.

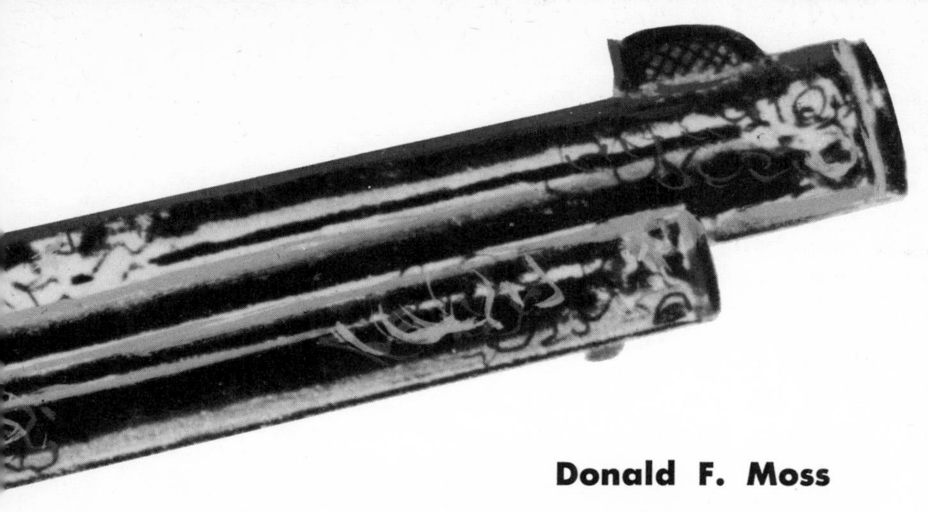

Donald F. Moss

Free-lance Artist

"Hot as a . . ." was a sketch assignment to render a pistol that would complete the caption esthetically and quickly. It was suggested that it be an engraved model with inlaid gold for color and richness. With this in mind the comprehensive was rendered with a plastic-like quality forcing the color and design for fast readability. After client approval, the comprehensive was ready for finished art.

After calling the Colt Manufacturing Co. in Hartford, Connecticut, I was invited to visit their plant and select the pistol desired. I chose three valuable models: a Colt 38-caliber six shooter — the famous Peacemaker — a priceless signed model with gold engraving, and one for use in rendering the ivory grip.

The final painting was rendered in tempera and watercolor on hot pressed Whatman board with a predominantly warm palette. The actual pistol, the Peacemaker, was set up under a fixed spotlight arrangement on my drawing table. In keeping with the headline, "Hot as a . . .", I used a piece of brilliant red paper to reflect on the pistol to heighten the dramatic effect. The result was a painting closely related to the comprehensive but with an authorative accuracy and color strength that made it a powerful 24-sheet poster.

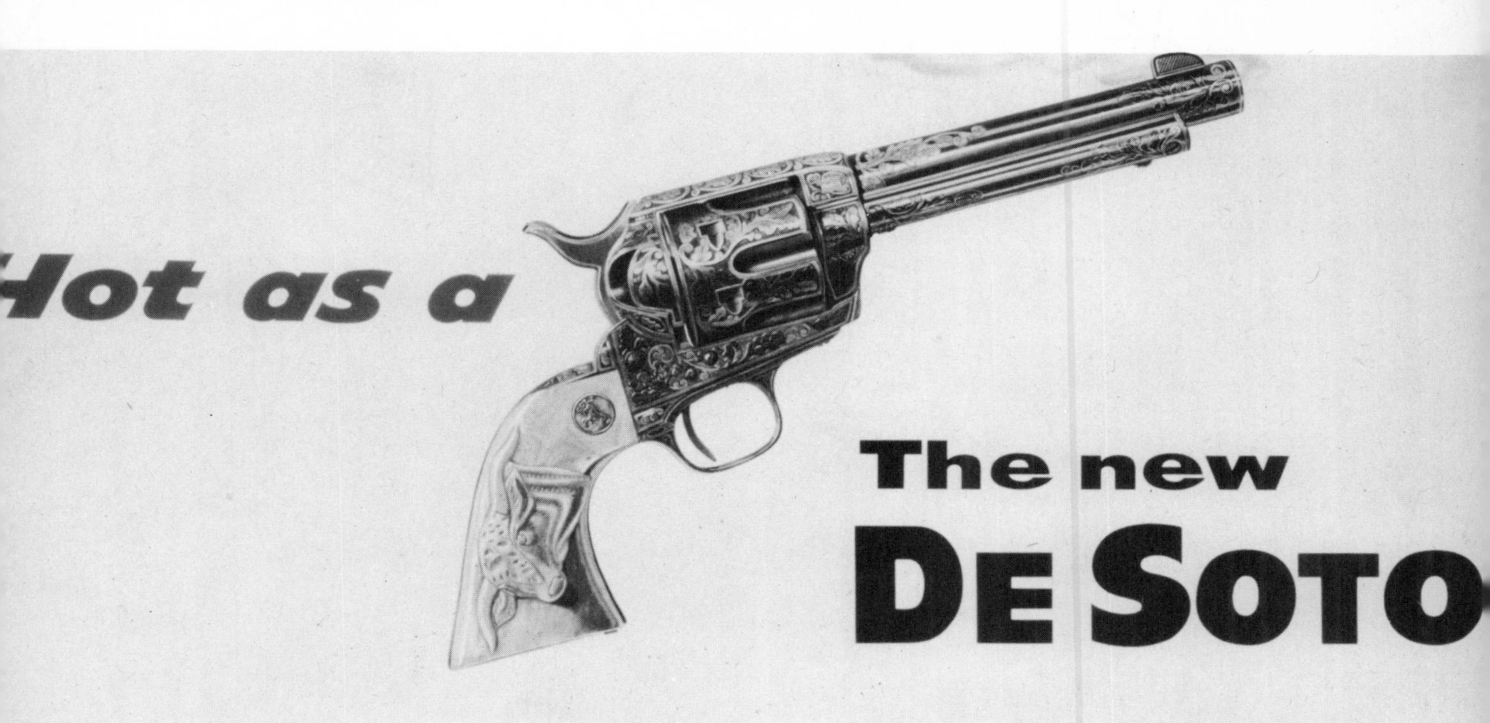

James A. Ernst, *Sketch Artist at Batten, Barton, Durstine & Osborn, Inc.*

A decorative free-flowing line is highly individual. The approach may be purely decorative or it may be humorous. Line drawings of this nature may be used for features, backgrounds, or spots. The Gillott pen point No. 290 was used in the drawings shown here. It produces a fine line and is flexible. For a slightly heavier weight, No. 270 may be used. The evenness of line depends entirely upon control. The pen may be handled as one would handle a pencil although in a slightly more upright position. And the weight of line depends upon the pressure applied. For a continuous free-flowing line, the key pencil drawing, set down first either as an underlay or on the surface, should be used only as a guide. The less restricted the preliminary pencil drawing, the more freedom of movement is allowed for the pen. It may take a series of trials before the artist produces a drawing he likes.

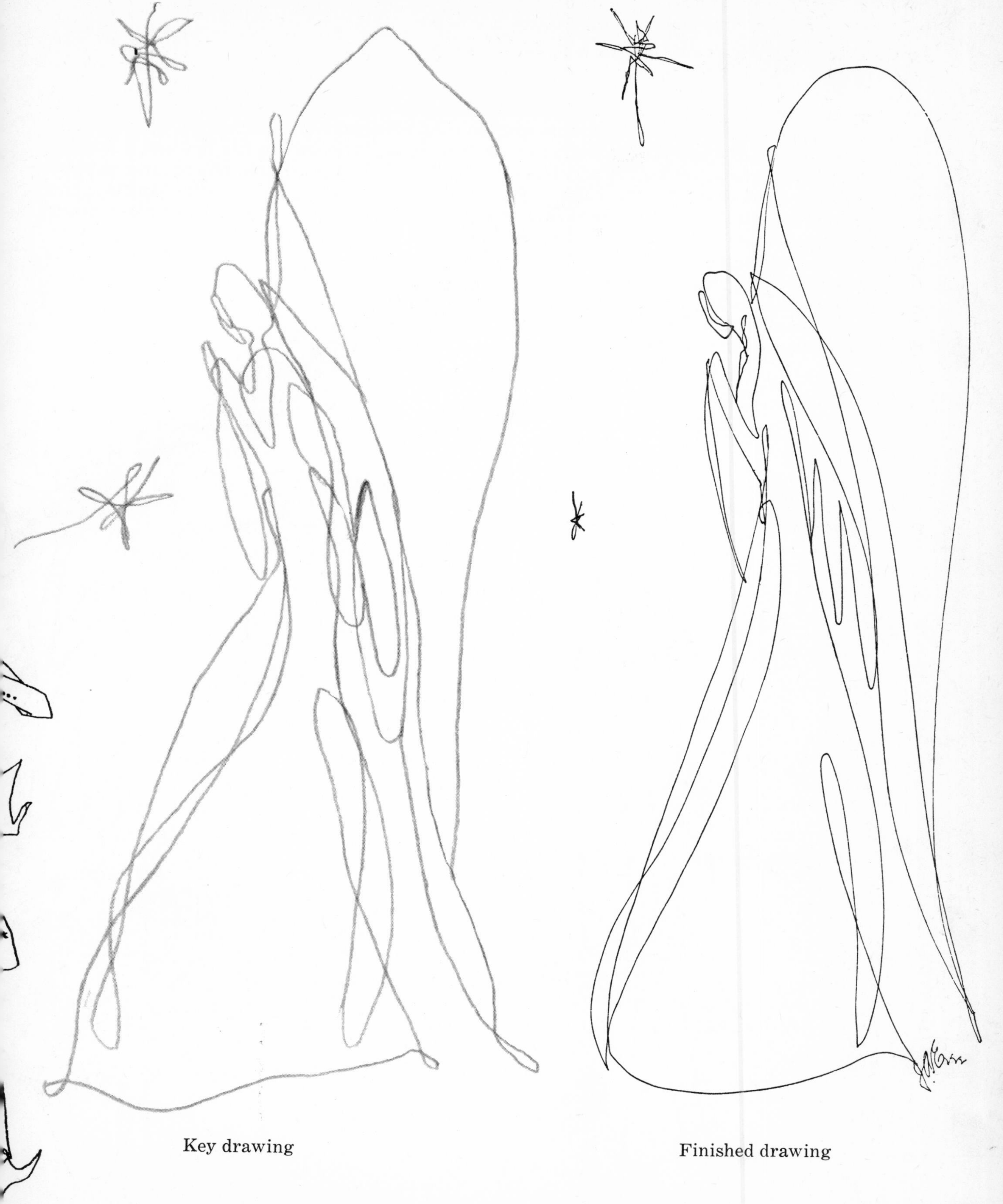

Key drawing

Finished drawing

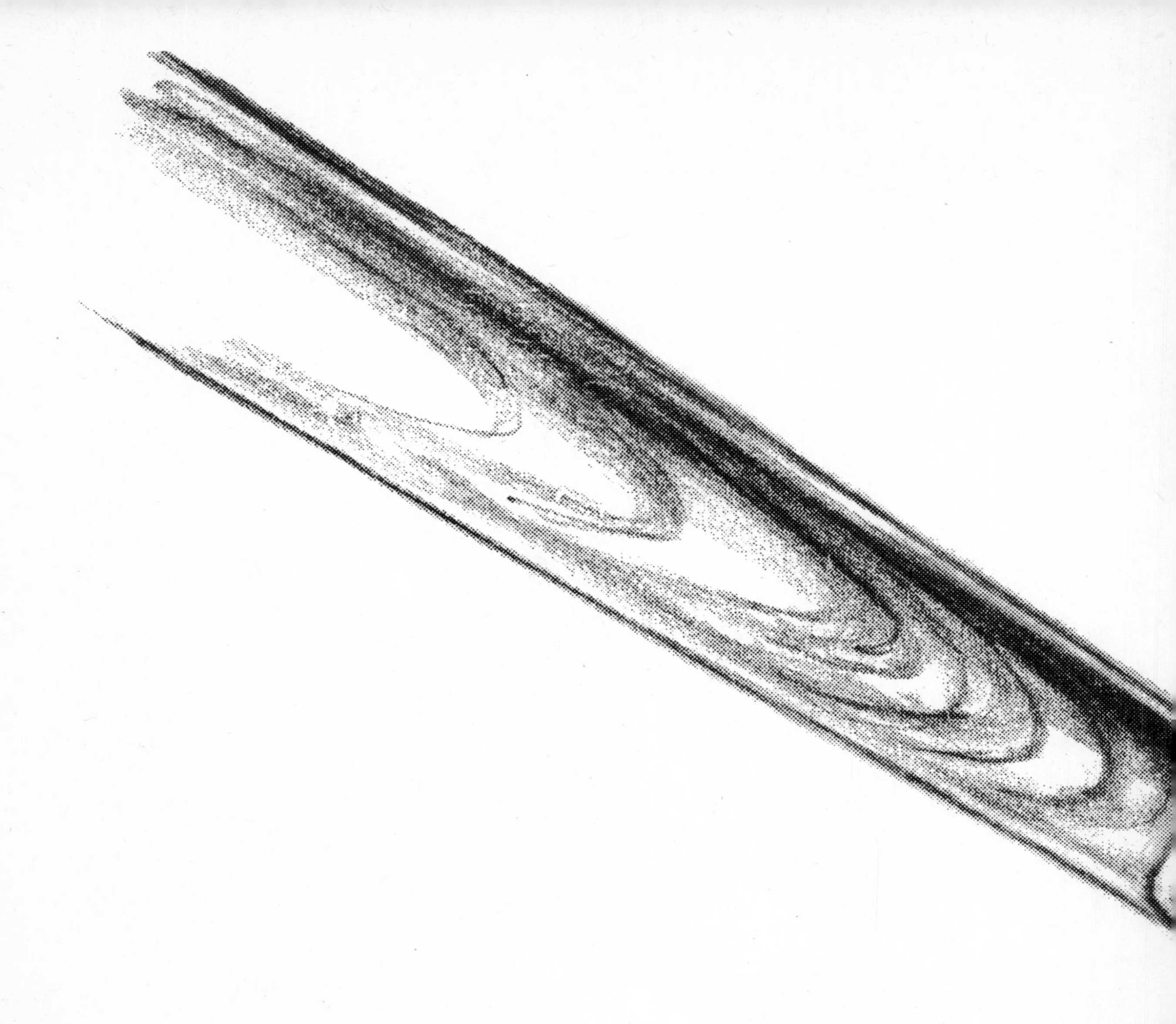

August Bleser, ***Sketch Artist at Batten, Barton, Durstine & Osborn, Inc.***

You have read a great deal in these pages about techniques. Often the subject itself dictates the proper handling of the problem. The surface you work on is of equal importance with the medium. In the illustration above we were after vigor and dramatics. We wanted a rugged quality suggesting a surface with a good tooth. We chose a dark Nupastel for the drawing, put it down boldly, and left it alone.

Walt McGovern

Art Director at
Batten, Barton, Durstine & Osborn, Inc.

The final selection was the fellow third from the right. He's a pleasant chap who lends an air of dignity to the product . . . and yet isn't beyond loosening up once in a while.

/HO WOULD LAST THE CAMPAIGN

Speaking of loosening up, it is interesting sometimes to use charcoal or Wolff's pencil instead of India ink for a finished drawing. I make them three or four times up in size to compensate for the added weight of the line.

George Rapp, *Free-lance Artist*

In both of these sketches the essential elements are daintiness and high fashion.

The treatment of the man's suit was kept very flat and dark as a contrast to the dainty, high-keyed quality of the girl. Color contrast is achieved by using deep cold gray as opposed to the girl's warm color.

In the sketch of the lady-in-waiting I kept the area around the satin skirt dark and flat to offset the shimmering effect of the material. A simple front light helps to carry the dark tone from the lower part of the picture up the back to her head.

To Every Lady-in-Waiting

Your baby can be spared skin problems that were thought to be inevitable

MENNEN
baby
powder

Art Director's rough

Seymour Ball, *Sketch Artist at Batten, Barton, Durstine & Osborn, Inc.*

The art director's quick rough, above, is intended as a guide to the elements desired in the picture, the size of the panel, and, roughly, the action of the figures.

In the comprehensive sketch, above right, the interior perspective, scale, and drawing of figures is worked out with a reasonable degree of care. The drawing was done on tissue in charcoal and Wolff pencil, first in outline, then strong blacks where desired. Blacks take better before the surface has been sprayed with fixative, which is the next step. Tone is added with charcoal pencil rubbed with a stump to get rid of excessive granular texture. The fixed underdrawing remains as a guide which can be erased over and stumped without disappearing. Then a final fixing is applied.

Working on a slanted drawing table, you will find that a great deal of charcoal dust sifts down

Comprehensive sketch

the sheet. I fold up the bottom inch of paper to catch the dust and keep it out of my lap.

In the finished illustration, at the right, you will note a few changes in the figures, requested by the client when he approved the comprehensive. The workable plan of the comprehensive was then carried to a successful finish by the outside artist.

FASTEST!

TWA's SUPER-G CONSTELLATIONS

NON-STOP **ST. LOUIS** DEPARTS 8 AM

Here is not only the fastest but the finest service ever offered to St. Louis. Your plane is TWA's magnificent new Super-G Constellation—world's quietest, most luxurious, long-range airliner. Inside the spacious cabins you enjoy the finest food in flight, superb service, unparalleled comfort in specially soundproofed interiors. And it's all yours at *no extra fare!* Enjoy it on your next trip to St. Louis. And remember, TWA also offers many other First Class and Sky Tourist flights daily to key cities across the U.S.A.—including non-stop Super-G flights to New York and one-stop, one-plane flights to Europe.
Super-G service to St. Louis begins March 1.

Hear WALTER WINCHELL Sundays 6 p.m. KHJ
Brought to you every week by TWA!

PHONE: MIchigan 8141

See your TWA travel agent, call or visit one of TWA's conveniently located ticket offices:

540 W. 6th Street • Hotel Statler Lobby • 6201 Sunset Blvd. Hollywood Roosevelt Lobby • Huntington Park: 2612 Saturn Ave. Inglewood: Los Angeles Int'l Airport • BEVERLY HILLS: 9482 Wilshire Blvd. CRestview 4-6661 • BURBANK: Lockheed Air Terminal, THornwall 8-4437 • VAN NUYS: 14437 Victory Blvd., STate 5-0428 PASADENA: 698 E. Colorado St., SYcamore 5-4141 LONG BEACH: Wilton Hotel Lobby, HEmlock 6-9691 WHITTIER: 114 E. Philadelphia St., OXford 4-2664 • SAN BERNARDINO: 373 Court St., 8-7922 • SAN DIEGO: 213 Broadway, BElmont 3-0131

Fly the finest... **FLY TWA**

TRANS WORLD AIRLINES

U.S.A. • EUROPE • AFRICA • ASIA

Completed ad

Rolf Klep, *Free-lance Artist*

On these pages we take a relatively simple technical illustration for analysis. This is the second of two which appeared in *Collier's* to illustrate an article on miniature submarines. The research involved getting information on the latest type of mini-sub, evolving a helicopter of size sufficient to lift at least ten tons, devising a cradling gear that would carry the submarine and be able to raise and lower it while the helicopter was hovering, showing a carrier of recent design with the correct equipment on its deck and bridge.

Having worked with the client for many years, I do not have to show "tight" comprehensives; talking roughs suffice. These, unless otherwise specified, are executed in soft pencil and/or pastel over the last of the successive pencil roughs evolved on transparent layout paper. This presentation — also

on transparent layout paper — is photostated to the required size and is used for any required checking, for the publication's layouts, for preliminary tracing of the finished painting, and for the artist's key to color. It is a rapid way to produce a presentation without losing the time required for the more intricate technical details appearing in the final illustration. Apropos of this, you will notice certain changes and much more detail in the finished painting.

Should certain minute details or labeling be required on the sketch, the pastel is blown lightly with fixative, the detailing applied with brush and opaque watercolor, and the sketch given a final coating of fixative to prevent rubbing.

Patrick J. White

Sketch Artist at Batten, Barton, Durstine & Osborn, Inc.

We are conditioned by our background and experience. Having been an art director, I tend to think of sketching from an art director's viewpoint: as a projection of his idea in the most direct way, achieving the mood of the illustration with an economy of means. I try to hold my sketches to a minimum of lines and tones, stating only the essentials, leaving the rest to the imagination. A free handling of light and shade is substituted for a strict deference to true shadows. The *effect* is the thing.

This method, of course, is not applicable in every case. Several factors are involved in determining how far a sketch should be carried. Some clients have the ability to visualize the finished ad from a rough sketch; others demand a tight comprehensive for their endorsement. The solution varies with each problem.

DU PONT
Cellophane

Henry McAlear, *Sketch Artist at Batten, Barton, Durstine & Osborn, Inc.*

In these full-color Nupastel sketches my procedure was to work from dark to light. Thus the full range of available values was determined from the beginning. Correct values rather than subtle color I find most important in carrying a sketch, with the three main groups — darks, grays, and lights — kept distinctly patterned.

The tones were laid on boldly side by side with the softening and blending held to a minimum until the final stages. It is surprising how little adjustment of edges is required when the values are laid on correctly — eliminating the murky effect of too much working over.

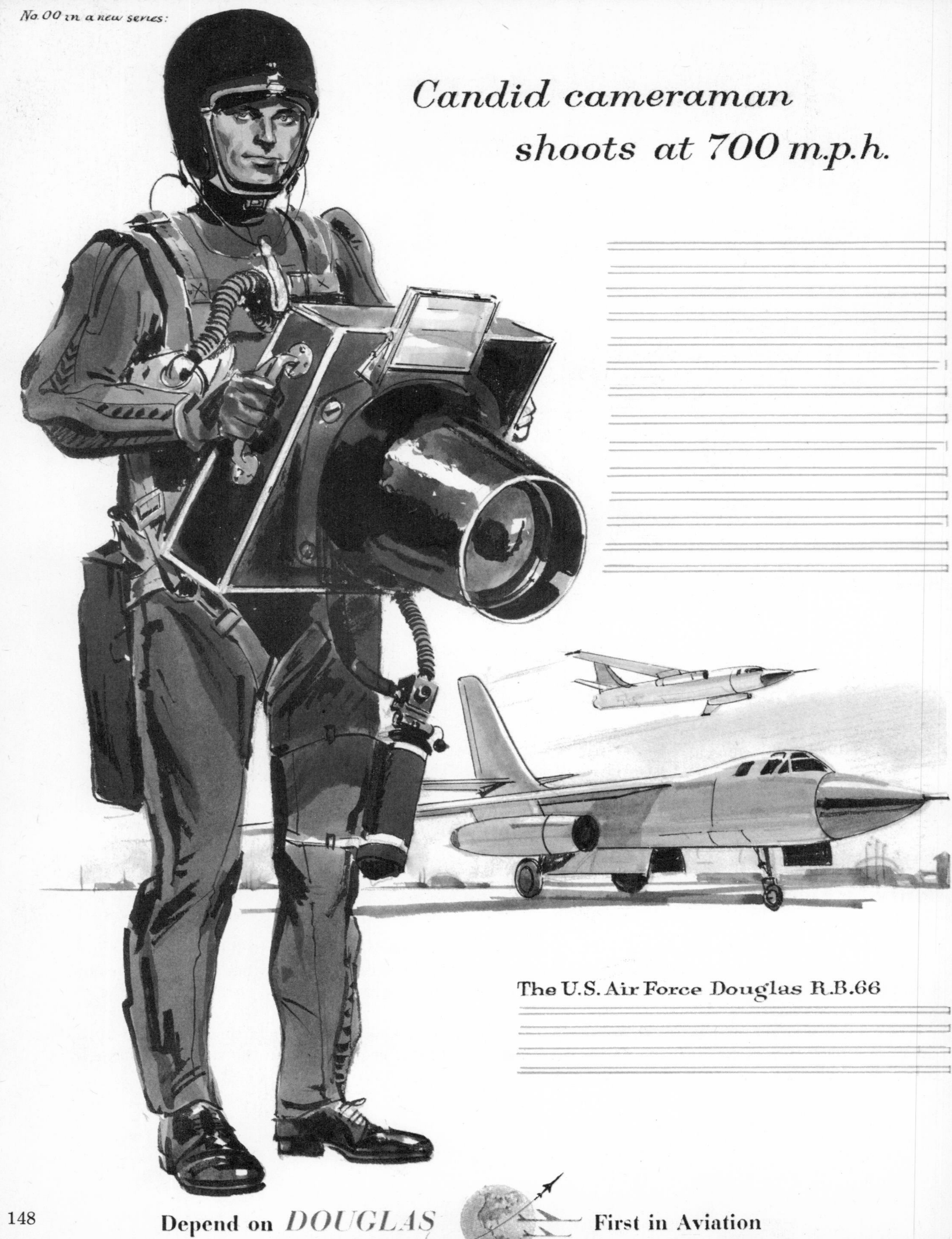
No. 00 in a new series:
Candid cameraman shoots at 700 m.p.h.
The U.S. Air Force Douglas R.B.66
Depend on DOUGLAS
First in Aviation

Edward Klauck, ***Sketch Artist at J. Walter Thompson Co.***

Every advertising agency is faced with the problem of the finished comprehensive. This problem must be met on large accounts in which many different personalities and departments of the client must be satisfied. Since in many cases the representative of the advertising agency is not always present to explain or defend any and all of the many facets of the illustrations in an advertising, the rendering of these pictures must be self-evident. In other words, many personalities besides the advertising manager may have a voice in a campaign, and if officials inexperienced in the terminology of the advertising business are to pass on these presentations, the agency will avoid any misunderstandings by making the comprehensive as finished as possible.

This type of comprehensive is usually done in watercolor or the medium that will most closely represent the finished art work in the final proof. Generally speaking, the artists who do this work are men who have previous experience as finished illustrators and therefore are better equipped for this type of comprehensive. They qualify because of their ability to compose and carry out illustrative problems without the use of models and with a minimum of preparation, since in most cases there is not enough time.

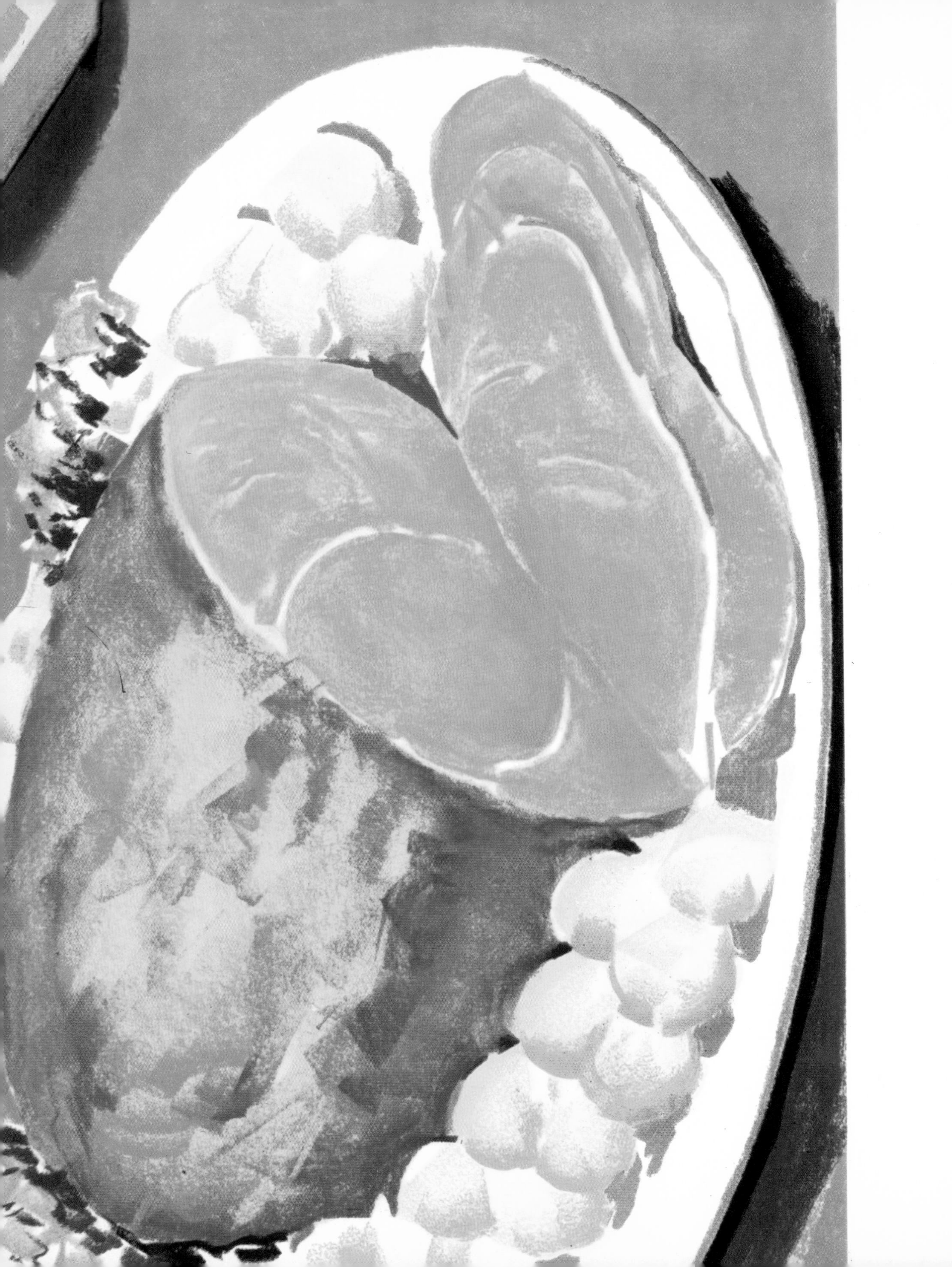

Still Life of a Ham

Here is an interesting example for you to try rendering with your set of Nupastels.

First, apply a light tone over the top of the ham using yellow No. 257-P. Apply this color with the flat side of the stick. For the more browned edges of the ham, about an inch wide, use No. 233-P. The sharp corner of the stick will give you a sharp edge. Then rub the yellow lightly to enrich the color. For the open end of the ham and the slices, use No. 286-P. Combine this with a light overlay of No. 243-P, which is slightly warmer in color. Use No. 239-P for the gray shadow on the plate and No. 205-P for the background color. For the darkest accents in the ham use No. 213-P, and No. 263-P next to the potatoes. In rendering the potatoes, use the sharp corner of your stick to retain a crisp edge, using No. 247-P for the light side of the potatoes and No. 243-P for the shadow side. Use all color except the dark browns lightly. Do not apply color so that the tooth of the paper is filled. Rub the colors lightly when you want a soft blend. By doing this, each color retains its own character and yet has a soft relationship to the other. Above all, do not over-model — try to complete each unit with one stroke!

The Importance of Research

When you are assigned a particular job to render and have all the important information pertaining to it, it is well to spend some time acquiring any photographic copy or scrap that will help in doing the best job you can do in the time allotted.

For instance, the United States Steel TV ad on the left represents no particular place, but it has the flavor of the copy I used. The actual scene was put together from several pieces of copy. The sleigh and horses were developed from a pencil sketch I had preserved in a sketch book. When the clients were shown the comprehensive (which had been prepared with an overlay for the necessary lettering), they liked it so well that they decided to use it for the finished art work. This is not unusual; sometimes just a little more work done on a sketch makes it a finished job.

On the following two pages are three churches, used by the Bankers Trust Company of New York City for their 1954 Christmas cards. I had to study these churches for the right lighting to get the best results. They were photographed in July, and the snow was mentally visualized. These sketches were also submitted as comprehensives, but were liked so well that they were reproduced without a change. The actual size of each watercolor is 6½ inches x 9 inches.

(Negative plates courtesy of By-Barton-Cotton, Inc.)

The Church

St. Mark's-in-the-Bouwerie

nsfiguration

St. Patrick's Cathedral

Sad Sack

Here is an interesting exercise for you to render in pastel. It was done with a set of Nupastels. The following colors with their respective numbers will help you in reproducing this example.

First, use an underlay — No. 243-P; be sure not to be too strong in applying it however. Then rub it *lightly* with the finger. For the red tones use No. 213-P. The very darks should be applied next, using No. 263-P. Use black for the nose and mustache, and red in the mouth, No. 206-P. Leave white paper in the highlights of the eyes and on the tip of the nose. Do not rub or blend too much, as you will destroy the grain of the paper, which gives texture to your drawing.

Baby Heads

Both of these baby heads can be rendered by following these pastel numbers, applying them as stated.

For the general all-over tone on the light side, use No. 276-P. The rich pink half-tone is made with No. 286-P. For the shadow tone under the chin use No. 212-P and No. 233-P, for the cheek shadow No. 213-P. For the hair on the upper head use No. 204-P and No. 283 for the bottom head. For the shadow in the ears use No. 296-P.

In rendering any head of this size, do not bear down too heavily on the paper, as you will completely fill the tooth of the surface of the paper and the next application of color will only slide along the surface of the other color. Remember, the white of the paper is your white medium. Do not destroy it by carelessness. Always experiment on a separate sheet of paper to see what effect you will be getting.

Whenever you have dark areas in a rendering, always apply those first, then add the other tones. Try these suggestions as you read about them and you will see immediately what the results are.

In pastel, any pigment on the surface of the paper will only tend to lighten up any dark color. If you have used a darker color than you should have, it is impossible to get a clean light value over it or get the color clean. If you want to take a large color area out, apply rubber cement over the surface and let it dry. Then remove it with a cloth wrapped around the finger or use a rubber cement "pick-up eraser."

Rendered from photographs by Constance Bannister

A Last Word of Advice

As I have stated on various pages, there are many ways to render a comprehensive sketch. Each advertising agency has its own policy as to which direction to take in making a layout. One agency may favor wash drawing; another, pencil; still another might use the Cado pen. It is a long road to master any of these mediums, much less all of them. The artist who experiments the most, who constantly draws anything and everything and uses all of the mediums mentioned herein, will be making the fastest progress. There are no short-cuts in acquiring this knowledge. However, if you will practice the applications as illustrated in this book and follow the advice given, I am sure you will improve your efforts a great deal faster than if you had learned the "rendering tips" I have included in this book by hard experience. It is my sincere hope that *Rendering Techniques* will give you that advantage.

Index